ISLAM
The Seed of Slavery?

ISLAM
The Seed of Slavery?

by

Rev. Maiwa'azi Dan Daura, C.H.O.

Understanding the spirit behind Islam —
A revelation that demands
immediate attention
and an urgent response.

VINCOM PUBLISHING COMPANY
Tulsa, Oklahoma

ISLAM - The Seed of Slavery?
ISBN 0-927936-91-7
Copyright © 1996 by
Rev. Maiwa'azi Dan Daura, C.H.O.
Prevailing Faith Ministries International
No. 5 Constitution Hill Road
P. O. Box 1826
Jos, NIGERIA
011-234-73-54569

Published by VINCOM PUBLISHING CO.
P. O. Box 702160
Tulsa, OK 74170
(918) 254-1276

Contents

Foreword

By Carlton D. Pearson

My first meeting with Reverend Maiwa'azi Dan Daura was an interesting and quickly arranged encounter. My wife insisted that I meet him, because a friend of hers, who had been a missionary to Nigeria, had Reverend Dan Daura minister at her church. She knew that he was coming to Tulsa and asked for me to meet with him. I wasn't really sure why I was going to meet with him, but my wife was insistent, so I did.

We had been talking for only ten minutes when I realized (by making inquiry of him) Islam's impact on Africans. I had already been doing some research on slavery and the enslavement of Black peoples in America and its origin on the continent of Africa. I wanted to verify that African slave trade to the West originated with Islamic merchandisers. *"For the love of money is the root of all evil..."* (1 Timothy 6:10 KJV) — and in some instances, the *lack* of money. We always seem to stop with or at slavery, considering it the major opposing culprit. However, you will realize through reading this book that it is as the Scripture says, *"For the love of money* (not money itself) *is the root of all evil...."* I always say, "While you cannot serve God and money, you can serve God *with* money."

Deep into our conversation, I realized that Maiwa'azi knew something by *experience*, and right away I asked him if he would be willing to write his experience down so we could publish a book, making this information available. We prayed, shook hands, and he left my office saying that he would do this. To be honest, I didn't think he would, and certainly not so quickly. But he did get the information to me. It was very well written and was exactly what I wanted and more, most enlightening and informative. We believe this is a God-ordained venture. I have learned so much from him in just our brief encounter and look forward to a long and fruitful relationship with him in the Holy Spirit and in ministry.

Two years before the Iron Curtain was torn in two or the Berlin Wall crumbled to the ground, before Peristroika, Glasnost, or even the release of Nelson Mandela from twenty-seven years of incarceration by the then apartheid South African government, the Archbishop Benson Idahosa of Benin City, Nigeria, warned me prophetically that Communism was on its way out and that the next great so-called "evil empire" on earth would be the dramatically increasing rise of Islam. Since that foreboding prediction by the powerful Nigerian apostle, I have noticed with great interest a new boldness and almost wild and arrogant display of Islamic world leaders begin speaking out against and even threatening to bring down the so-called "Great Satan" of the West, which is primarily a reference to the United States of America.

Living in the United States causes one to occasionally draw comparisons to other countries, many of which differ greatly from the United States, and many have an ongoing feud with the entire Western world.

My first encounter with — or introduction to — Islam was neither the Sunni or Shi'ite branch, but a sort of hybrid off-shoot called "The Nation of Islam," which was, at the time, headed by the late Elijah Mohammed.

When I was just a kid in the sixties, our community called this group "Black Muslims." I was always distantly intrigued by these stern, no-nonsense, clean-cut, young Black men, neatly dressed, usually in dark suits and handsome bow ties. The older people, most of whom were Christian, always warned us younger folk to "stay away from them ol' Black Muslims." For the most part, we did feverishly avoid their repeated solicitations to buy either their newspaper, "Mohammed Speaks," or their relatively inexpensive, mouth-watering bean pies. At that time they seemed fairly harmless. However, since those days of my youthful innocence and ignorance, I have discovered that Islam, both the "Nation" as it is referred to here in the African American community, and orthodox Islam, more predominant outside the United States (especially in third world countries), is a far more serious and confrontive, even combative, religion than most of us ever realized.

Today, thousands of Black people, many who were raised in the Christian church, are flocking to that spirit. Even people who continue to call themselves Christians are uniting themselves with a false prophet. Paul said, *"The Spirit clearly says that in the latter times some will abandon the faith and follow deceiving spirits and things taught by demons. Such teachings come through hypocritical liars, whose consciences have been seared as with a hot iron"* (1 Timothy 4:1-2 NIV). Of course, false prophets don't usually realize that they are false prophets, but when you *are deceived*, you *will deceive*. Although the Word of God is clear, too many of our Christian preachers seem afraid to address this issue. However, nearly 2,000 years ago, Jesus Himself addressed what is happening in our country and around the world today.

> *"For then there will be great distress, unequaled from the beginning of the world until now — and never to be equaled again. If those days had not been cut short, no one would survive, but for the sake of the elect those days will be shortened. At that time if anyone says to you, 'Look, here is the Christ!' or 'There he is!' do not believe it. For false Christs and false prophets will appear and perform great signs and miracles to deceive even the elect — if that were possible. See, I have told you ahead of time"* (Matthew 24:21-25 NIV).

I have noticed that Islam dominates large parts of the African continent — affecting countless millions of my precious Cushite ethnic family. Lately, I have developed a rather serious interest in the effect of this complex and mysterious religion's impact on particularly dark-skinned peoples and cultures of the world.

When I compared rates between Arab dominated countries (i.e., Libya, Iran, Kuwait, Lebanon, etc.) to African dominated countries (i.e., Somalia, Niger, Sudan, Senegal, etc.), the rates for death, violence and poverty were considerably different. In places like Nigeria, Bangladesh, Pakistan and other Central African nations where the dominant religion of the government is Muslim, life expectancy rates and the literacy rates are lower than Arab Muslim countries with similar stated religions. And incidences of killings by authorities, political detentions and imprisonments, political unrest and non-political torture reports are considerably higher than in non-Black Muslim dominated countries and cultures.

One of the most profound and interesting discoveries I made in my research, which is verified in this book, is the history of Islamic oppression and enslavement of Black peoples from as far back as the fifth and sixth centuries A.D. Responsible research and historical records will make it formidably and increasingly apparent that Islam has exhibited a considerable amount of racism and prejudice toward Africans, East Indians and other dark-skinned or Negroid people around the world.

Protestant Christianity, on the other hand, though far from a perfect religious experience, has statistically reflected a significantly different and more positive impact in countries where it is the dominant influence. While these statistical differences vary and can be the result of any number of variables, in addition to or besides Islam, I think it merits at least some investigative thought and inquiry as to why these differences exist. Further study will reveal that the mystical side of Islam, which includes numerous forms of voodoo, sorcery and witchcraft, has resulted in massive genocide (including starvation) and other forms of violent and senseless extermination and slaughter of millions of people, both non-Islamic and Muslim.

The numbers are alarming and cause for some careful and prayerful thought, and even spiritual and political action. The Scripture says, *"In fact, everyone who wants to live a godly life in Christ Jesus will be persecuted, while evil men and impostors will go from bad to worse, deceiving and being deceived"* (2 Timothy 3:12-13 NIV). I hope this book will open many unsuspecting eyes, hearts and minds to a heretofore unaddressed phenomenon within the Cushite and/or Hamitic peoples of the world.

This book, in effect, is a wake-up call to the Church: "Blowing the trumpet in Zion, and sounding an alarm on God's holy mountain" (Joel 2:1).

Introduction

Islam, with its million and one never-ending schemes and ways of panel beating and structuring a man, holds the world's greatest population of adherents only next to Christianity in number. The religion which originated from Saudi Arabia spread forcefully into Africa, Asia and Europe. It is strongly missionary in outlook. It is also the most resistant of the non-Christian religions to the Gospel message. It proclaims no final gift of salvation but an ambiguous salvation by works through the observance of the regular prayers, giving of alms and tithes, being good, the Ramadan forty-day fast and pilgrimage to Mecca at least once in a lifetime.

No one is doing any organized intelligent effort towards reaching the Moslem world with the true Gospel. The Middle East is basking with all kinds of wars and struggles and counter-struggles because of the gross darkness covering the land. If Africa was a dark continent before the Gospel era, then the Moslem world today is the darkness itself. The light of the Gospel is as distant or totally non-existent in 99 percent of the Islamic world. This presents a wonderful challenge and opportunity for the evangelical movements worldwide.

This book was written from the Biblical perspective, reinforced by well over twenty years of experience working in Northern Nigeria, which is the very seat of the powers of Islam in the sub-Saharan Africa. Having lived in the practices of Islam, it was no difficult effort trying to open up the inner bellies and weaknesses of the system to help the Moslem outreach evangelist with dynamic tools for radically and thoroughly reaching the most difficult ardent Muslim activist. This is a personal testimony. An eyewitness account of a true encounter with the forces of Islam.

Honestly speaking, great obstacles exist but they are totally surmountable. With sufficient manpower, willpower and prayer power, the Islamic world will be the mission ground for tomorrow, next to Russia and China.

Areas of conflict and differences were fully explored, investigated and treated. Scriptures commonly abused and blasphemed by Moslem interpretations were also given appropriate attention.

If you intend to become a responsible Christian, then this material is meant for you.

It is proper here to acknowledge noteworthy people who, by one way or another, made this book possible. I want to thank Rev. Carlton Pearson by whose major help this book was able to see the light of day.

My sincere thanks also go to Rev. Selbut Longtau, Abraham Ajibade and Lani Stephens for their help in researching and collecting information; Mrs. Edith Temlong and Binta Audu for helping to put the manuscript on disk. My thanks also goes to those of you who will, after reading this book, start doing something about conquering the world of Islam for Christ.

Rev. Maiwa'azi Dan Daura, C.H.O.

1
The Man Who Would Not Die

The Local Beliefs

My father, Dandaura Samu Ngbinrin, was born sometime in the late 1920s to a purely animist family. As he grew up, he started hearing of the appearances of the ghosts of long dead relatives at the village water stream which was its main water supply. Every family, no matter how well placed, had to go down to this stream for their drinking, cooking and washing water. There was no other alternative.

One particular morning during his childhood, they went down to the stream to wash and get some water. They met a man buried from the top of his head to the soles of his feet in the very sticky mud of the stream, lying there unconscious. They left their water-fetching utensils and ran back to the village to get help. When the man was removed from the mud and restored back to consciousness, he told of his ordeal with these ghosts. He was returning from the farm late in the evening, everywhere was dark and he was alone. While he was trying to cross the one kilometer width of the stream, he met with these two skinny but powerful beings. They did not look like human beings but looked like walking skeletons. They moved with the wind and spoke with wheezing sounds which only they understood. It looked like one of these beings desired to enter into him, but he sternly resisted.

In that process, a hot chase ensued. He ran in all directions for dear life. The more he ran, the more confused he got until he finally lost consciousness, but he could remember falling; and as by a miracle in the subconscious level, he could now understand what these beings were saying in the wheezes. They said since it was beginning to be daybreak, they should bury him in the mud away from where he could be discovered so they could return the next night for him. The ghost talked of how pleasant it was to live as human beings in the village, and desired earnestly for a return to the village to live as humans and eat the food they were used to eating while alive. That was the last time the man spoke. He lost his voice and became a useless person locally.

Stories were told of other ghost appearances that would embarrass women sexually and even molest small girls. People also mysteriously disappeared at odd hours at this stream, while others met with very strange happenings.

Someone told of walking down a lonely pathway in the village and without any hand, heard a very hard slap on the side of the jaw after which his mouth lost alignment and moved about sixty degrees to the side. His eyes also moved about the same sixty degrees and, of course, the rest of the face moved by the same shifting.

In his youthful days, it was normal to watch a local village fight at the village square where all the eligible bachelors displayed their strength and wrestling guts. To be able to outdo your opponent and give him a total knockout, you needed the help of a local native doctor who either "cooked" or "baptized" you with some local concoctions made out of a mixture of varied herbs or different animal parts or a mixture of both. It could take a young man up to five years to receive enough cookings or baptisms of their local herbs just to prepare him for his wrestling bouts of the future. To make victory at the first entrance into the wrestling arena double sure, it was not strange to have charms of all sorts secretly buried in the wrestling arena long ahead of time and also take a certain dose of the concoction all day long. Then, when the D-day comes, you dress your wrestling glove with all kinds of knockout charms. Some of these charms were supposed to make your opponent giddy as you give him either upper or lower cuts on the face. All of this was simply to make a daring impression on the most beautiful lady available for marriage at the time. She was always for the taking of the champion of the duel. The faster the knockout, the stronger the impression, because the lady is assured of a strong husband who can protect the home in the future against external aggression since intermarriage and inter-tribal wars were a constant occurrence. No one really would like to give his daughter to a coward who would run away from the home when someone who has been eyeing the wife comes into the home to take her by force.

It was also no rare occurrence to trick a girl and give her some sweet drink containing love portions to capture her heart and love. It was said that when this was done to either a boy or a girl (since both sexes practiced this), the one who is charmed loses her/his will, his/her ability to choose is weakened, his or her resistance capacity is totally wiped out. The administrator of the charm will be in total control of the charmed individual. He controls the person at will as one would control a zombie; no other influence can break the charm except the one who administered it or a more powerful native doctor, much stronger than the one who prescribed the charm.

The Local Champion: The Moslem Imam

It was in the midst of all these situations that my father grew up. So he started searching for the best charmer he could find. He was introduced to quite a number of quacks, who proved unsatisfactory and almost disastrous. However, he kept on with the search. So, one day he met a Moslem scholar who told him about his Quranic teacher who could do anything. You name it and he has it. He was said to have the ability to communicate with spirits. He could give charms that would keep you from dying by accident or by charms, curses, or incantations made against you by another witch doctor.

He was said to give a vanishing **"Kampe"** (this is a leather parchment made into an underwear). If you enter into the wrestling arena wearing this "Kampe," you could become invisible. When your opponent would reach out to hold you, you would vanish. And from that spirit vantage point you could beat your enemy within seconds. *In fact, it was widely speculated that this Moslem imam would not die. The spirits had given him an everlasting life.* This was so tantalizing to the young man who needed only small protection and some small championship favor.

So, he met with this mallam or imam who lived in a well-scented house. His scents had magical powers in them. They were said to have the ability to ward off "evil" spirits. Evil stood for any spirit that would not favor the candidate or use such scents. Most of these scents were hung on the door posts of the entrance of the house. Herbs used in some of the scents were also planted around the house to grow as flowers.

When my father met with this highly acclaimed imam, his instruction was to repent from animism, the worship of idols which was a requirement for this champion charm-giver to use as a springboard for his operation. His charms worked best only after one became a Moslem by "baptism" and declaration of "la-illa-a-illala-mahamadu-rasullilah," meaning Allah is one and Mohammed is his only latest prophet.

Since my father needed all the power he could gather, he went through the rituals of the baptism and the declaration. He was then renamed "Dandaura," meaning son of Daura. (Daura is a town in Northern Nigeria.) That day he was made to drink the ink washing of some special Quranic verses written out on an "allo" or slate which is specially cut out to look like a Qur'an, and is used for adult literacy and the writing of Quranic recitation verses.

My father literally became a disciple of this imam. He would spend much of his time with this scholar who taught him both the structure and practice of Islam. He taught that

Mohammed always told his followers that Allah said "tashi in taimake ka," meaning Allah helps those who help themselves. To this Moslem imam, this meant, get all that you can get to protect yourself, to promote and provide for yourself and leave the rest with Allah. And the new convert, a young man, believed this to the last letter. So, he took all the charms this imam could give.

Some of the charms were made of Quranic verses written on leather parchments and sown together into small wraps and then wrapped around by black animal hair. These were called either "laya" or "guru," depending on what they were meant to achieve. Some of them were meant to protect the bearer from harm or hurt by the bearer's enemies who would try to attack in any way. Some of the "gurus" were meant to bring good luck. For instance, you could get a "guru" who would give you special favor to sell your goods in the market if you were a trader, or give you a good harvest if you were a farmer.

This champion imam also had the ability to call rain, thunder and lightning against those who were rivals of his confidants. He could "Ja yasin" or "Ja aya," meaning to create bad omens by the recitation of some special incantations or a special mystical Quranic verse.

My father continued with his Islamic training under this "wise" instructor. To him he had found a pot of wisdom. Years came and passed. With every passing moment, he found himself believing more and more on this mallam as he saw his exploits and omens come to pass. He came to really believe this man was untouchable, even by death. A man who could make things happen, a man who could speak to the spirits, who on earth could take his life? He was therefore worth all the attention, zeal and commitment. Anyone could feel safe with such a person.

By now my father had been fully Islamized and the champion imam, chief charmer, had become his little "god" and great mentor. He followed all the Islamic instructions meticulously and carried all the charms and scents preciously. He had found a great treasure of power, and he was not about to give it up. Neither was he ready to compromise with any other religion or religious practice that would jeopardize his new-found faith and opportunities of greatness. His mentor was nicknamed "mallam sharubutu," meaning "the teacher who drinks much of Quranic slate verses." He was known in the Keffi local government area of the present plateau state in Nigeria as the champion of Quranic recitations. With this great feat, he was believed to be untouchable.

This man had the ability to read minds from a distance. If you lost your goat or dog, he could tell you who stole it, how it was stolen and where it was taken. So he had a quick way of dispensing justice to the local populace. Since he could tell who the thief was, he could also identify who was wrong in most basic matters, such as family fracas, group misunderstandings, dowry settlements and the like. He was highly patronized by both Moslems and animists. People who went to consult with him were first and foremost given a brief rundown or summary of their lives with dates and gravity of some occurrences in their past. Without revealing their secrets to him, he knew it from his spirit's contact. Then they would also be told of their future and how to prepare for forthcoming events. Young men would go in to be told who their wives would be.

Oh yes, my father needed to know who his wife was going to be. He was made to serve with the greatest dedication in prayers five to seven times a day. He was literally chained to the system of the mallam's belief. He was enslaved to the mallam, what the mallam represented and his religion. But he had one problem. All his religious observances, prayers and rituals could not keep him from the *movement* of lust, pride, anger, jealousy and envy he felt constantly in his heart. It looked like his friends in the church had a different spirit. There was a *settling* about them. They were peaceful. A special wind of calmness and laughter was all over them. They seemed to have conquered immorality and greed. But for him and even his mallam, he noticed a lack of consistency.

In spite of the rigorous religious observances of the imam, he still had so much attachment to worldly things.

The mallam would not travel out of town without his praying mat and a kettle or jug of water. He observed all his prayer sessions, even if he was traveling along with other passengers. The lorry must stop when the time to pray arrived. He would wash his feet, hands, ankles and hair in preparation for each prayer. It was such a job just to prepare to pray. It looked like the Christians did not have to do that. They seemed to enjoy free entrance to God and could talk to Him with such ease without having to take any special position or face any special direction to pray. Yet they had more joy and peace. They spoke with such a certainty concerning death and eternity. But our mallam just spoke of the powers he had and how nothing would kill him. He knew little or nothing about death nor did he know how to prepare for it. Neither did he care or know much about eternity. His life was lived only for the now. But my father was filled with all kinds of thoughts concerning death. His animist relatives died. He had always wondered if, when you died, it was all finished. Something told him it could not be so.

In spite of all the powers that mallam possessed, in spite of the fact that he had four wives, the mallam seemed to lack the power to keep himself from illicit deals with other people's wives and even young underaged girls. It looked like mallam was possessed with a strange demon of lust. When queried about his strange passion and his uncontrollable sexual desires, he said "Allah" understands and has allowed it to be so. Otherwise, all those evils would not have happened. Such was the mind of the Moslem imam.

Mallam was also a slave of some other deadly habits. He had strange fits of rage. When he got mad, everything around him would fly in a million and one directions. He behaved like one really possessed by some angry spirits. His wives were a most miserable lot. They dared not be caught in the web of his anger. Of course, any little offence met with beatings and terrible curses. It was not strange for all four wives to be crying at the same time from beatings. Most of them lost all their incisors and canines. In bad cases, some of them would be beaten into unconsciousness. His children feared him like animals would fear a hungry lion in the forest. He screamed at them and lashed out at them all the time. They did not know gentleness, meekness, kindness and love. They were hard, rough and mean because of the treatment meted to them by their father.

The mallam always had very deep remorse at the end of each reckless episode of meanness. He would always wish he had the power to stop doing such mean acts. The very things he hated were the things he always did. The things he loved, no matter how hard he tried, he could not find the strength to practice. So the spells of wickedness continued unchecked. The champion of power, the great imam could not find power from his spirit or his inner energy to heal himself of wickedness. He had all the Islamic religion he could get. He had all the prayers Islam prescribed for a man of his religious status. He discovered that all of these were not enough. There was need for some other external power intervention — a power greater than the power of his spirit, a power greater than the power of Islam. But he was too proud, too bound up to seek for the power he saw manifested in the Christians around him. In his secret confessions, he always confided in my dad about the strange power at work in the Christians.

He also confided in my dad that of all powers, it was only the Christians' power that his spirit was always afraid of dealing with. The power at work in the Christians was too much. Each time he sent an incantation or a curse or some sickness against them, all he saw was a thick, bright light which also burned with contact.

The great mallam had a strange power mirror which he used in summoning whomever he desired to harm. It works this way: When you report to him that you desire to kill some fellow, after the appropriate incantations, he would then look intensely into the mirror and call the victim's name.

He kept a jar of water by the side. When the victim appeared in the mirror, he simultaneously appeared on the water. He then used a knife or a sharp dagger to stab him in the heart, liver or brain. The victim would bleed right then into his jar of water. Physically, the victim would only feel a sharp stab. He could even fall down suddenly unconscious or dead. In some cases, he would become ill and subsequently die. He had killed people by this means literally thousands of times. Even if the victim was a million miles away, he would appear on the mirror anyway.

One day this mallam was given the name of a child of God. Unknowingly, he made his incantation and called the name, but the believer did not appear. He screamed the name almost a hundred times, but the supposed victim would not appear. He was mad with his medium spirits. He summoned those medium spirits, but they refused to appear. Later in the night, since he could not sleep, the medium spirits came and told him never again to collect the names of those kinds of people because these people were friends of the Holy One. He asked who this Holy One was. The spirits simply told him, the God of the Christians.

When mallam called the name of the believer, the medium spirits said, "The Holy One stood up for him. That was why the believer's shadow did not appear on the magic mirror or water." The spirits said, "Moreover, we had a terrible blowout with the Holy One before, and our master was terribly wounded. For this reason, we avoid Him as much as possible. Do not call the name of anyone connected in any way to the Holy One again!"

It was about 2:30 a.m. when the medium spirits left. The mallam could not sleep. He wondered about the greatness of the power of the Christian God. Daybreak came and life continued as usual, and mallam kept on with his religion and religious business of charming and bewitching people.

One day someone had a fracas with an evangelist. This fellow ran to the mallam and complained. Mallam took the name and then went straight into a cursing session. The magic power mirror was brought out, and the jar of water appeared by its side. The mallam poured some powder into the jar of water to make it super strong. He then called the name of the evangelist. Suddenly, the face of someone who had long hair and the most beautiful eyes, nose and mouth appeared. A dazzling light appeared all around the face, and it had piercing power. The mallam could not look straight into the mirror nor the water. The man simply said, *"Do My prophet no harm."* This voice was authoritative and convincing. The voice had a deep echo as this beautiful man spoke. When he was through speaking, the mirror suddenly splashed and broke into powder pieces, the water immediately dried up and both the mallam and his client were left blind. They could see nothing for seven days. The spirits he called upon did not appear until after the seven days. They told him they kept away because there was too much power in the house for those seven days. They repeated their previous warnings, which he neglected, and told him that any further mistakes could be fatal.

Mallam continued his business. He was too attached to his religion to see this higher power that broke his magic power mirror. He had such a strong, persuasive speech. He was eloquent and had a sharp, piercing tongue. He was anointed by the special powers of his medium spirits to speak and convince and bring people to submission. He was empowered by the spirits with the ability to control people and make them do things. Chiefs and emirs could not do without him. So real was his influence that his fame spread all over the territory. He was held in such high esteem that no one believed he could die. How could a man endued with power to kill others die?

In fact, the man had the power to speak to the dead. One day a woman came with a request to talk to her late (dead) husband, so the mallam took her into his chambers where he practiced necromancy quite often. All lights were put out, and they sat in front of a bowl of cold water. He made his incantations and called out to the dead man, who immediately appeared and was seen over the bowl of water. So he asked the woman to speak to him. She saw her husband and recognized him. She received answers to all her questions. After she was satisfied, the dead disappeared. The woman left from the necromancy session. When she returned home, she felt a very strong presence in the house. She went to bed that night but could not sleep. Suddenly, things in the house started moving. She could hear footsteps walking towards her and then away from her.

Since she was so frightened, she went back to the mallam and reported it. He gave her some scent to burn in the house. He told her the things moving in the house were "Iskokai" or demons who move with the wind, and she should not fear. He said that after she burned the scents for a week, they would all go away. But the demons would not go away. All efforts to send them away failed until she went to a pastor and told him of her experience with the imam. The pastor told her Christianity did not believe in the appearance of the dead because it has been appointed unto man to live once and die once, after which follows the judgment of God.

Man dies and cannot appear in the world in any form until after the judgment. The woman confessed she saw her husband. The pastor told her that the demons that were haunting her house took her husband's face and appeared to her to deceive her by pretending to look or speak like her husband. He prayed a simple prayer with her after which all the visitations by witches and demons ceased.

And the Man Died

One day my dad went to see the imam, this great mallam, the powerful charmer. He knocked at the door. Instead of the usual voice of the mallam, it was the voice of one of his wives who answered from behind the curtain. He requested to see the mallam. The wife of the mallam said, "Mallam is gone on a long trip." She asked my dad to return in two weeks, "For by that time mallam may be back."

After two weeks he returned, anxious to get some wisdom from this imam, but the wife told him mallam was still not back. Someone who met him at the entrance of the house took him aside and told him mallam was not just gone on a long trip, he had acutally died and could not rise up again.

Conversion

An American missionary came around often to talk to my father about Christ. But because of the stranglehold of his imam, he had no breathing space to see clearly and make a choice between Islam and Christianity. The news of the death of his powerful imam spread. So the missionary came and reminded him of what he told him earlier about Christ. He had told my father that his imam would one day die and would have to face Christ. Christ, he said, is alive and would never die because He died and rose again after three days.

My father, however, equated the missionary's Christ with his own Islamic imam. He argued that his imam, too, would not die, and if he did, he would rise again also.

When the missionary visited my father after the imam's death, he reminded him about Christ's eternal life. He also told him Christ was anxious to share this eternal life with my father. If he believed, even if he died, he would live again. This was very tempting and convincing, so my father capitulated and gave his life to Christ. The missionary then discipled him.

He was severely attacked and ostracized by his Islamic comrades, and he had to move a hundred miles away to find his place and stand in the Christian fatih. He has set up over thirty local churches since his conversion and is actively working towards doing more.

Going to Islamic Literacy Program

After I was born I grew under the Islamic influence. All my friends were committed Moslems in childhood. We attended Quaranic recitation classes where the mallam (or teacher) taught us how to recite verses of the Qur'an. This would continue until our early teens. During the classes, we learned the Arabic rendering of the Qur'an. The teacher was quite mean. Any slight distraction attracted hot lashes from the horse whip. A child of about six years was whipped one day until he lost one eye. Someone had his ear torn up. This was the norm in the society within our limited Islamic setup, that as children we had to attend school. Otherwise, I felt like bolting away to save myself from losing an eye. To learn the verses and to be able to recite them, we needed to know the vowel sounds of the alphabet and then learn the words step by step.

When this was over at about the age of eight, we were taught of the areas of conflict between Islam and Christianity. These differences supposedly proved that Islam was the only religion that believed in one god, so it was considered the surest medium of genuine, godly worship.

These areas of difference included:

A. *Internal contradiction of the Christian Scriptures.*

The Christians see the Qur'an as a confused composition of crude writing which lacks cohesion between sentences; a collection of inchoate and irrelevant ideas, which lack persuasive charm. The Moslem sees his Qur'an as the only god-given final revelation to man. It has also remained untouched by change and susceptible of no alteration. Mohammed said he got his "inspiration" in two main ways:

1. At times Gabriel spoke the words to him as one man would speak to another.

2. At other times it is likened to the ringing of bells, which penetrated his heart. This affected him most.

We were taught of the internal evidence for the authority of the Qur'an in Sura (chapter 32:13), which proved its inspiration. Mohammed got this "inspiration" (revelation) over a period of twenty-three years. After his death, these revelations were compiled and recorded from written annotations on stone tablets, camel's bones, leather, parchment, papyrus and from oral sources. By 650 A.D., all compilations were completed.

We were also taught that the Christian Scripture was abrogated with the entrance of the Qur'an. "If this is so," they argued (which to the Moslem it is solemnly so), "the Christians have an unauthoritative Bible, and only the Qur'an holds God's latest revelation to man." They taught that the 600-year gap between Christ and Mohammed presents a vivid ground for the belief in the Christian Bible abrogation. We were told that Jesus said He was going to send a Comforter after He was gone. Mohammed supposedly was that comforter.

Even though Mohammed carefully denied any suggestion of his own supernatural character, Moslems still insist on making him some super-human. Mohammed saw himself only as a man liable of error. He said, "I am the mouthpiece of the revelation of Allah." And he claimed to be nothing else. In Qur'an Sura 80:11, the book states that the Qur'an is "an admonition on noble, lofty, pure lives through the hands of noble scribes." So the book was revealed through a noble but human scribe.

The Qur'an, however, calls the Bible:

- "The book of God" (Sura 5:48).

- "The word of God" (Sura 2:70).

- "A light and direction to men" (Sura   6:9).

- "A guidance and a mercy" (Sura 6:155).

The corruption of the Christian Scripture, however, is a belief held by Islam that runs parallel to its views of abrogation. We were taught that the Bible has often been changed, transcribed over and over by less than scrupulous scribes. Therefore, it most assuredly needed to be superseded by a more current straight-from-God holy book. The Qur'an of Islam was that book. To them Allah corrected all the wrongs in the Bible in the perfection of Qur'an.

There were almost a dozen Quranic verses teaching on the corruption of the Christian Scripture, some of which include:

1. *"Woe to those who with their own hands transcribe the book (i.e., corruptly) and then say, This is from God, that they may sell it for some mean price" (2:73).*

2. *"O people of the book! why clothe ye the truth with false-hood? Why wittingly hide the truth? (i.e., by covering up part of the text; e.g., with the hand while reading) (3:64).*

3. *"Some are there among them who torture the scriptures with their tongues, in order that ye may suppose it to be from the scripture, yet it is not from scripture" (3:72).*

4. *"The ungodly ones among them changed that word into another than that which had been told them" (7:162).*

In comparing the Scriptures and the Qur'an, every honest reader will discover that the writer of the Qur'an was greatly influenced by the Judeo-Christian religions. It is generally believed that Mohammed got most of his Biblical knowledge from the intellectual environment of Mecca. But we were simply taught that Mohammed was inspired of Allah through the chief angel Gabriel to pass on Allah's uncorrupted word to the world.

B. *The Doctrine of the Trinity.*

The second area of conflict we were taught was the Christian belief in the Trinity. To a Muslim, you can be assured of a most emotional atomic bomb blast. We were told it is an abomination to say God had a Son, for God is one. Christians are said to have perverted the pure mono-theism of the Jews into a corrupt polytheism. For this we were told the wrath of Allah would be upon the Christians and all their generations. Things are even complicated further by the worship of Mary. If you want to be stoned to death, then talk about the Trinity in a Moslem environment. The Qur'an most assuredly declares and affirms God's unity.

> *"Say; He is God, the one on whom all depend! He begetteth not, and he is not begotten, and there is none like him" (Qur'an Sura 112:1-4).*

Mohammed felt very deeply about this subject. "They have said: The merciful hath taken to himself offspring, ye have committed a thing monstrous, at which almost the heavens are rent, and the earth cleft asunder, and the mountains fall down in pieces: Because they have attributed to the merciful offspring, when it does not behoove the merciful to take to himself offspring" (19:11-73).

"Believe in God and His apostle and say not 'three' — for hear! It will be better for you — God is only one God" (4:169). Other Quranic teachings concerning the Trinity include:

> *"They surely are infidels who say, God is the third person of three, for there is no God but one God: and if they refrain not from what they say, a grievous punishment shall light (on them)" (5:77).*

> *"Lo! Allah forgiveth not that a partner should be ascribed unto Him" (4:48).*

It is interesting to see how the Qur'an sets Jesus up to deny the Trinity as He dialogues with God:

> *"God shall say, 'O, Jesus son of Mary, has thou said unto mankind — take me and my mother as two gods besides God.' He shall say 'Glory be to thee! It is not for me to say that which I know be not truth'" (5:116).*

We were told the pagans believed in all kinds of gods. There were father gods, mother gods and son gods. The Christian Trinity, they say, is not too far from such paganism. Examples of these could be found in the moon god, the sun goddess, and their son from a trinity religion in Ancient Arabia. Ea, Marduk, Bigil are represented as father, son and intercessor in Babylonia. India puts forth Brahma, Rudra and Vishnu as absolutely invisible; with these examples, the Moslem finds it hard to believe or comprehend the Christian Trinity. The Moslem fails to understand that the

Christian does not worship the Trinity as three Gods, but one. No special worship mode is prescribed for the Father, Son and the Holy Ghost as with the pagans. One sacrifice of the Son was all the Trinity needed that man may be reconciled to God. But it's not so with the polytheistic pagan trinity. Each god required his own kind of sacrifice to be appeased. Pagans have their gods cut out of wood or stone or some other graven image, but not so with the Christian. He does not believe in emblems or idols of the Trinity.

The Christian sees unity within the Trinity. The Trinity is handled with an awesome quietness and reverential faith. The deep-seated mystery of the Godhead is veiled within the counsels of God. Man will be given full and final perfect revelation of this mystery when all is put under His feet and Jesus takes His place as King of kings. No matter the smartness of the genius of man, no matter the intelligence and technological breakthroughs, man still will not be able to understand the mystery of the Godhead, because man is trapped in a limited body. He can only understand things his frame allows him to understand. Man's limited body can therefore not understand things wholly or perfectly, but partially. Even if God had chosen to openly manifest all of Himself to man, man will still not be able to comprehend, until the day man is given that immortal body that in its constitution shall be like God Himself. For we shall all be like Him when we see Him face to face (1 John 3:2).

The well-trained Christian therefore knows that to convince the unbelieving about the Trinity will not be a matter of arguments and contentions. But it will be by being confident of his own stand personally, by dwelling less on the metaphysical details and more on the spiritual significance for life which the Trinity symbolizes. It is God Who convinces the hearts of men. Powerful prayers from holy hearts bring conviction to the unbelieving.

C. *The Cross.*

The highest and greatest misunderstanding is found in the message of the cross where the Christians say the God-man died on the cross by the hands of mortal men. How contrasting is the prominence of the cross and its provision of salvation for all mankind in the Bible compared with a crossless Islam, which makes an effort to offer man redemption on the basis of personal merit only. The Christian approaches the cross with the reverence and solemnity of a devout worshipper, while the Moslem, through ignorance, profanes the Holy of Holies by his vehement, vicious attacks on this central pivotal work of God.

For the past century, the cross to the Muslim has been a symbol of cruelty and carnage. To the Moslem, the cross is the very antithesis of love!

The informed Moslem, taught and schooled, believed to the end that Christ was too much to be killed on the cross by mere men. It's an abomination and an anathema to say the prophet of God with the powers of Christ could ever be handled by man. We were taught from the Qur'an Sura 4:156 that:

> *"And for their (i.e., the Jews) saying, 'Verily, we have slain the messiah Jesus, the son of Mary, an apostle of God.' Yet they slew him not and they crucified him not but they had only his likeness. And they who differed about him were in doubt concerning him: No sure knowledge had they about him but followed only an opinion, and they did not really slay him, but God took him up to himself."*

Actually we were taught that while the soldiers were about crucifying Christ, He suddenly slipped off and gave Judas, who betrayed Him, His face and semblance. So when they were nailing the man to the cross, they thought it was Christ, but Christ was long gone to heaven. The concept was that Jesus was an apostle of God. The cross was only meant to kill those accursed of God. Jesus therefore couldn't have died on that cross.

When Jesus escaped from the hands of the soldiers, He was translated to another country where He got married, lived and died a natural death.

They taught us that success was the mark of any

great person. How then could One sent from God have been subjected to the most cruel and degrading of all deaths?

The Qur'an in Sura 3:48 supports the idea of a natural death for Christ.

> *"Then God said, 'O Jesus, verily I will cause thee to die, and will take thee up to myself and deliver thee up to myself and deliver thee from those that do not believe.'"*

The Ahmadiyya movement believed differently. They believe that Christ was really crucified, but He only fainted on the cross, was taken down and left for dead. He revived in the cool of the night in the tomb and then commenced a journey to the east through Persia and Afghanistan, ending up in Kashmir. It is believed that Christ then preached until the ripe old age of 120 years when He died and was buried in Srinagar, where His tomb can be seen even today.

The death of Christ on the cross is a mystery. To those who are perishing, the cross is foolishness and a stumbling block to the Jews and as folly to the Greeks. But, in reality, the cross is the "power of God to those who are being saved." Remove the cross from the Bible, and you have destroyed the power of the Christian message forever.

Someone once said:

> *"The cross is the center of all revelation. Have you ever thought what the Bible would be like without the cross? Take the cross out of the book, and you won't be able to recognize it. If there be no promise of the cross in the testament, then its laws distress one. It is then a book of fatalism.*
>
> *If there is no cross in the New Testament, then it blazes with pitiless splendor. Put the cross back, and at once the book becomes a Gospel. Its law becomes love; its shadows flee away; its destiny is the Father's house. To reveal my sin merely would load me with despair, to forgive my sins merely would make me afraid of tomorrow. I want my sin conquered; I want to get it beneath my feet. The cross is the place of victory. Christ achieved it on the cross. I say it reverently:*

He could not do it but for the people. He had put away sin, all sin — original sin and actual sin — by the sacrifice of Himself. There was no other good enough to pay the price of sin. He only could unlock the gate of heaven and let us in. Education could not do it. Social reform cannot do it. Our beautiful essays and ethical sermons cannot do it. It is Christ upon the cross Who discovers sin, Who forgives sin, Who conquers sin."[1]

At the intermediate level of our Quranic school, we were properly indoctrinated with the behaviors becoming of any proper Moslem. Islam was to occupy the supreme office of our lives. All our decisions must be considered in the light of how such decisions will affect Islam or a brother Moslem. The five pillars of Islam were to be at our fingertips. Five prayer sessions a day were mandatory. Whether these things changed our lives or not, they were to be strictly observed. If any prayer session was missed in the day, one had to pay. Islam thoroughly affected every detail of life with its prescriptions and requirements. Islam totally and quickly eradicates the culture of all converts upon whom it imposes a totally foreign and new lifestyle, ways, customs and language. Every other custom is viewed as being devilish and must be purged from every convert or conquered. An imposing mosque will be erected at the most central location, and the "call to prayer" sounded at every appropriate hour.

We were taught that all Moslems were brothers. This was a constant thought forced down your throat, resulting in a brotherhood solidarity that is impregnable by the outsider. The foundation for this unity is a fanatical devotion to Islam, which basically combines faith and patriotism into one unified force and thrust. This is why a Moslem who converts to Christianity is branded a traitor to his nation and an infidel apostate of Islam.

After Mohammed had converted an Arabian tribe, whose consecration included absolute devotion to family and tribe, he made the tribe an enlarged brotherhood, linked together by religion. In the mind of the Muslim, an organism emerged from this unity between family, tribe and religion. This organism is seen as a body which cannot permit severance of organs or members from itself. For a Moslem to repent and be converted to Christ meant that he is an apostate and has been cut off from the body. He is seen as one who had denied the faith of his fathers or ancestors. And to deny one's father's religion is to invite social ostracism. Total loyalty to family, tribe and religion is expected of all Moslems, so a breaking away from it calls for violent treatment.

In training, the teacher or imam has total powers. Whatever he says is final, as if it is the voice of God. Unfortunately, these men are normally old-fashioned, unsociable, uneducated and seriously, extremely fanatical in their views. Therefore, the trainee moves in an area of intolerance, fanaticism and bigotry. He becomes almost mechanical in the performance of religious duties. The Moslem is not allowed to question, investigate, or analyze anything he is taught. Islam is void of any personal dynamics.

In the traditional Islamic setup, after conversion, if such a convert decides to recant and forsake Islam, he then becomes liable to execution under the law of apostasy. Authentication for the severity of this act is to be found in the following Quranic passage:

> "Whoso shall apostatize from this religion, let him die for it and he is an infidel" (Sura 2:214).

All apostates, as stated in Muslim law, consist of the abjuration of Islam by speaking words or committing acts that are incompatible with faith in Allah. Every attempt should be made to induce the apostate to repent. If, according to one jurist, within three days there is no return to Islam, then the infidel shall be put to death. Such is the cost that is to be counted before a Moslem becomes a Christian.

This law is the very reason why many Moslems fear to

come to Christ. It instills fear and great trepidation into the heart of any potential Christian-Moslem convert.

Anyone who embraces Islam embraces a bunch of hot coals into his bosom. It is a trap entered into too quickly without a way of escape. Within our society we have many Moslem converts who, because of the apostate law, prefer to remain underground. The severity of its sentence is the major cause why we do not yet see a landslide decampment of Moslems to Christ. (See the chapter, "Islam — the Violent Spirit" for details on violence done against converts.)

Islamic Brotherhood

Islam recognizes only a brotherhood of Moslems, not a brotherhood of man. When they say, "Peace be upon you," (Wassalamalekum) it refers to the peace of Islam. And technically you are not permitted as a Moslem brother to use the salutation with any other, except a Moslem brother. Every other person is an infidel and therefore is duly qualified for the wrath of Allah. Only those within the abode of Islam are Moslems.

The mechanical performance of duty serves as tie-in ceremonies. Fasts are performed simply because everyone is fasting, and to keep in the spirit of the brotherhood, you must fast, whether it means anything to you personally or not. No one dares to break his fast since this will attract the condemnation of the imam. The mosque is always open twenty-four hours and serves as a meeting point for all. The dutiful religious observance of all the five prayer sessions are a binding force. In Islam you live a communistic life as opposed to an individualistic life. There is a strong practice of a false spirit of deep reverence to Allah in worship, a hypocritical surrender to Allah, and a true lack of self-consciousness in witness.

In worship one is taught to concentrate, but all this is done hypocritically as one will be engaged internally in his thoughts with the immediate past activities, but physically could appear to be deep in worship. A Moslem uses the surrender to Allah as a means of subjecting others. When it comes to his turn to allow the surrender to Allah to keep him from making some irrational, emotional decisions, he first thinks of how the matter affects him. All the time, the Moslem finds himself reacting violently, aggressively and madly. It is only after such behavior that he remembers his surrender to Allah. The Moslem finds that he does not have enough self-control internally. The grace to be God-influenced is lacking in Islam.

Outbursts of anger are a sign of the Moslem brotherhood. In my relationship with fellow young Moslems, that was an all-day experience one had to either put up with or display. It was unbecoming for a young Moslem not to know how to fight for himself. Trouble was no strange lifestyle. You had to know how to take advantage of others. You could never be cheated, but rather, you could cheat others, especially if they were infidels. You are allowed to do anything to the infidel. Nothing can ever be too bad for a Moslem to do to an infidel. To a fellow Moslem, you were expected to protect your interest. With all these things in our minds, there necessarily had to be violent reactions in our daily lives to be able to win the best for ourselves.

Child Abuse

Because of the terrible lack of self-control, rape of very young girls in the Moslem schools is not a strange occurrence. By the age of between twelve and fourteen, when most Moslem girls get married, you can be sure that most of them have gone through all kinds of sexual abuse by older men. It is common to send girls between the ages of six and fourteen to sell and hock all kinds of stuff, ranging from already cooked food to raw food items. Most of them are seduced during the purchase of such items. Personally, I have witnessed all kinds of such seductions. A young girl will be asked to supply the items on sale to a secret place. Since she is usually weaker against the older, bulky man, she is then pinned to a life-threatening position and raped. She is usually left with the promise of marriage and financial support and warned not to disclose the event. In most cases, the small child does not go home to tell. Instead, she develops a habitual routine of supplying food to such persons who would normally pay quite well. Decency within the Islamic circle is far from reality.

The Origin of Christianity and Islam

Christianity originated in the area of the world that became the cradle of Islam. It was indigenous in the very countries in which now there is an emotional cry for the expulsion of Christianity, seen as the "strange religion." Christianity spread peacefully to Asia several hundreds of years before the militant Asian conquest of Islam.

Christ came from the land of Palestine, which sits in the same latitude and longitude as the Middle East where Mohammed comes from. Christianity was as non-Western, non-white as was Islam. The Gospel was more universal in application than was Islam, except that Christianity goes by peace, while Islam goes by militant force.

Yet through the centuries, Moslems have successfully and deceitfully represented the Christian faith as a white man's religion, which is completely alien to the life of the citizens of the third world. The results of their deception are evident — the wholesale capturing of the American Africans as converts.

The problem of the misrepresentation of Christianity has been increased many-fold by close identification of the white man's deeds with his religion. All white people are looked upon as Christians.Therefore, they find ample targets for their attack on a religion which produces a society of drunkards, immoral and decadent men. They have called on the evils of the white man's Trans-Atlantic slave trade of the black race as a Christian injustice done to the blacks. But they fail to tell the story of the Trans-Saharan slave trade, which was started and orchestrated by Arab Moslem traders and imams.

The Arab Moslems cunningly create the impression that the West is synonymous with Christianity. Therefore, the white man by definition is Christian. And it did not matter whether the white man was godly or demonic. The true Arab Moslem knows that Christianity came from the same vicinity as Islam.

It is good to note that Simon of Cyrene (Matthew 27:32), a black man, was in Jerusalem the day the final sacrifice to establish Christianity was to be made. Simon of Cyrene helped Jesus carry the cross to Calvary. He participated in the promotion of the vital instrument that was to give life and power to the Christian faith. The white man came into the Christian faith much later. Black Africa was known to have interacted a lot more with the land of Christianity than the white man. The queen of Sheba and the people from her area were dark-skinned. The eunuch of Ethiopia was a black man. God so considered the importance of this black man that Philip had to be forcefully taken away from the first-class revival he was experiencing in Samaria just to minister to the eunuch (Acts 8:26-40).

The Moslem whips up sentiments of the wickedness of the godless against people of other races. He tells the blacks that the white man has forced him to live for centuries with the humiliating knowledge that our color or birthplace condemned us to be second-class citizens. But the white man at least allowed the second-class citizens to live. It was not so with the Arab slave masters. Ample cases abound on testimonies of their treatment of the black race, holding them in great contempt as dogs, not as people. They were known to serve their slaves food on the ground just as they served their dogs food. The black slave in the Middle East never got freedom or release. The black man was not allowed to own any land, property, or anything of dignity among the Arab Moslem slave masters. The black man was killed, without regard of repercussions.

When our Nigerian pilgrims go to Mecca on a pilgrimage, unsatisfactory stories about their treatment by their Arab

Moslem counterparts are told. Our black pilgrims are treated with contempt and a separatist's attitude. They are given the worst campsites that are badly or shabbily organized and supplied.

It is good to understand that, though the Western nations have been privileged to enjoy centuries of Christian influence upon their culture and society, not all of its people have been controlled by the Christian culture. Christianity must be considered on its own merits and not on the merits of the white man. Just as there are godless Africans who are as wicked as Lucifer himself, so the West also has people who are godless and evil. We should not blame Christianity for this. It should be understood that because a man goes to church daily does not mean he automatically becomes synonymous with Christianity. All men may be liars, but Christianity remains as true and pure as it was the day Jesus died for it. We must be careful not to mislead our future generations because of some race's "inconsistent expected Christian behavior." We must be wise enough not to start behaving wrong while demanding that others straighten up. We must get right and straighten up as we apply the test on others. Remember, a man has no right to expect Christian behavior from another before he can consider Christianity as being authentic. Christianity should not be condemned because of someone else's behavior. Some of the white people are so young that they do not know the violence their Christian parents did to other races.

Islam should not be blindly embraced in protest to the Christianity of the white man. Islam must be properly considered, investigated, observed and understood before jumping on board.

Christians, whether white, black, red, brown or yellow, must lift up the banner of justice and fair play and fight against racism of any sort. The Christian Gospel is the total salvation of man — salvation from sin, sickness, oppression by Satan or man and deliverance from all forces and vices of wickedness. If a people refuse to be influenced by these whole principles, the Christian message which alone has the power to bring dynamic changes to a situation, must be preached soundly with clarity and conviction. For those who hold such a powerful Gospel as we know in Christianity to turn around and desire Islam, something must be terribly wrong. Should you be one of these people, you need to know more about Islam. By the time you know the spirit behind Islam, you will be better prepared to choose for yourself whom you will serve.

2
What Is Islam?

For the simple and the light-hearted thinker, the question — What is Islam? — expresses stupidity. One may say that Islam is a religion or faith proclaimed by a group of people.

Islam is a religion, it's a culture, it's a cult, it's a philosophy, it's politics and can as well be called a community, a definition most popular among political scientists and in international relations. Many more definitions can be given Islam, based on diversified social, philosophical, scientific, or religious perceptions.

To an extent, all of the above describe Islam, but I must declare that the ancestry of certain basic components make Islam what it is. They are:

1. Allah, the god of Islam.

2. Qur'an, the historical and material substance of faith.

3. Mohammed, the "ambassador" of Islam.

4. The Muslims, who are the disciples and professors of the faith.

The absence of any of the above components will definitely reduce Islam from what it ought to be, or kill it permanently. Remove Allah and there shall be no Islam; remove the Qur'an and there shall be no Islam; wipe out Mohammed and his historical deeds by disclaiming the Hadith as an authentic chronology of important events in his life and deeds, and you will have succeeded in wiping out Islam.

Now, I adjure you earnestly to open your eyes to the world all around you because this world is much more than the things it is said to be. Especially when it comes to this issue of faith and belief, certain things that may not have much scientific essence can still be probed by human common sense. An example is of the religion called Islam.

As an ex-Muslim, I lived as a Muslim with a neutral mind from birth. Most of the claims and testimonies in this book are first-hand, without prejudice or carnally subjective criticisms.

By definition, *Islam* means submission; i.e., a total, un-reserved surrender of oneself to Allah and His injunctions. The religion of Islam demands an earnest reverence for Allah, and there is no option for obedience when it comes to daily prayers.

Islam is a religion of self-righteousness, not of salvation that comes by the grace of God, like in Christianity. No Muslim can claim or prove assurance of salvation. They can never know how much of their good deeds will take them to heaven, so they must keep Allah's injunction paying *Zakat* (the tax) continually, going for *Hajj* (the holy pilgrimage), saying their daily prayers, fighting for and defending Allah. In fact, it is normal in Islam to pray for the dead this way: "The most merciful and most compassionate, we plead that you overlook all the evil deeds (probably including defraud-ing the state's treasury, shedding innocent blood, etc.) by mallam Abdullahi; we plead with you Almighty Allah to use his account of *good deeds* to justify him instead."

While Christians all over the world celebrate the free-dom from the law of sin and death, *Islam is known to be a religion under the law of Allah*. Almost nothing is done out of personal volition; not even the daily prayers. Everything is an obligation. There is no excuse for the ritualistic ablution that precedes the Muslim's prayers. The washing must be done. Otherwise, the prayers are not acceptable. Every law must be adhered to.

Furthermore, Islam is also defined as a *religion of peace.* What this means is that there is peace only among the people who accept Islam, and there is war against all who do not accept Islam. A congregation of Muslims is known as *Dar-es-salam,* which means *the house of peace.* The rest of the world is *Dar-el-Harb;* i.e., *house of war.* Patriotism and brotherhood are not defined by state, culture, values, or geographical location, but by Allah. And all other nations that do not acknowledge Allah are regarded as Dar-el-Harb (house of war).

Islam is a totalitarian religion. There is no borderline between economic, political and cultural values. Nothing is called democracy in Islam. A true Muslim leader is the one who can dictate and dominate his community, even if it means continual shedding of blood in order to hold the reins of government. This had been the pattern of Ayatollah Khomeini of Iran, Idi Amin of Uganda, Muhamar Gadafi of Libya, Ibrahim Babangida of Nigeria and other emirs and sultans among the Islam-dominated areas. Instead of Islam tolerating other gods or other kinds of opinions different from Allah's, they must fight to establish the kingdom of Allah on earth. Everything must be subjected and submitted to Allah.

Finally, Mohammed claimed that *Islam is a religion founded on five things*:

Shahada: Bearing witness that there is no god but Allah and that Mohammed is his slave and messenger.

Salat: Establishing prayer.

Zakat: Paying the wealth tax or alms giving. Since Mohammed was an orphan, he encouraged it.

Sawn: Fasting in the month of Ramadan.

Hajj: Performing the journey to the House.

These are some Islamic claims defining what Islam actually is, but we shall not stop here. We must relate to these claims. Of course, in the beginning of this subject, I already presented my personal analysis of Islam as a holistic system of tetra functional elements, which are *Allah, the Qur'an, Mohammed* and the *Muslims.* But for now, let us, as creatures of intellect, relate to some of the theological claims, theories, philosophies and practices as related to the human race. Even if most of Mohammed's manuscripts were lifted directly from the Old Testament of the Bible and a portion of the New Testament (as it is claimed), I understand, as an ex-Muslim, that the contradicting concepts of some Islamic theology about sin, righteousness, man/woman, heaven/ hell, marriage and satanic practices leave more questions than the points of consonance between Christianity and Islam. The teachings of Islam must be *properly studied* in order to ascertain its manifestos and its ultimate essence to mankind.

Historical Summary

Islam, as a religion, revolves around the principal actor, Mohammed, who was born in Mecca about 570 A.D. His father was Abdullah and his mother was Amina. His father died before he (Mohammed) was born, and his mother died while he was only six years old. At twenty-five, Mohammed married an older lady, Khadijah, who was forty years old, a very rich widow. It is believed that *Qur'an,* the sacred book of Muslims, was dictated to Mohammed by the angel Gabriel. Qur'an means *recitation.* However, the angel was delivering the messages from a single god who addresses himself in plural — his name was Allah. Allah could mean either the Almighty God, the Creator of the universe, or the god of Islam whom Mohammed introduced. I have dedicated a whole chapter to this subject.

In the Qur'an, Sura Ikhlas reveals Allah (chapter 112); Sura Qadr talks of the revelation of the Koran (chapter 97); and Sura Iqraa refers to Mohammed's call to recite the Qur'an (chapter 95:1-5).

When I was in high school, I never stopped referring to the Qur'an as an ex-Muslim. But this time, I saw more of Mohammed as a sensual, misguided poet, in whom the spirit of antichrist was deeply seated and enthroned. He was quite religious and disposed to eradicating the idols in Mecca, but his shallow understanding of Judaism and Christianity ended in an everlasting controversy with the Holy Bible, for which he had great respect. History tells us he was unlearned; hence, this could be his limitation from being a consistent and systematic philosopher. When he was forty, he received his first revelation and that was the start of the Qur'an.

I have talked about Allah, the Qur'an and Mohammed and now of Muslims.

The followership of Islam started with Khadijah, the prophet's wife. She could be excused to think her husband was hallucinating because of his attitude of going to secluded mountains to meditate and retiring to caves; but she encouraged the prophet when he wasn't sure if his first visions were demonic or divine. Another prominent convert was Abu Bakr, a rich man, who eventually became the first caliph who took over after Mohammed's death. The generation of these people were the first Muslims, not Abraham and Isaac as some blind scholars have claimed. This is the historical perspective in brief. Now let's x-ray the teachings, doctrines, practices and other values found in Islam.

Validity of Islam: Theology

Qiblah

Qiblah means the direction of prayer. In Islam there is a recommended direction one must face when praying or rendering any ritualistic exercise to Allah; otherwise, the religious "acts" would all be in vain.

The Qiblah for the Muslim is the direction of Ka'bah, the great mosque of Mohammed in Mecca. However, this wasn't the original direction Mohammed prayed and worshipped until a certain time.

In tradition, it is said that Mohammed worshipped at the south wall of Haram in Mecca, and could therefore face both Ka'bah and Jerusalem. One day Mohammed rose up to tell his followers not to face Jerusalem anymore, that their prayers would be in vain. He presented a new scripture from Allah concerning this. This act quickly alerted the Israelites to understand Islam as Mohammed's personal human effort to synthesize a hyper, super and self-fulfilling, counter religion against all other faiths in Jerusalem. Mohammed complemented this change of direction with a word from Allah to encourage the believers that he owned both the east and the west. The change of direction was only a test of loyalty to Mohammed and to distinguish the non-adherents who were to disown the prophet (Sura 2). So Moslems started praying facing the east.

Since this period, the entire Muslim populace of the world turn to Ka'bah. This is the symbol of unity in the Islamic faith.

However, it was obvious to Mohammed even then, that the unity in Christianity was not that of geographical location or prayer towards the "holy land." It was a thing of the Spirit. You could kneel, stand, whisper, cry out, turn to the north, south, east or west. Anyone who questioned the change of Muslims' Qiblah was thought to be foolish.

Satan

All over the world the devil or Satan has a single mask of *evil*, and in Islam it is no different. It is believed that Muslims also take the devil as an archenemy (Sura 35:6), but theologically, I question the personality of the devil (Iblis) Mohammed presented in *Baqara* (Sura 2:30-34) if it is the same spoken about in Isaiah 14:12-14. The offence committed by Satan in the Qur'an was *"not bowing down to Adam"* like all other angels did. But the doctrine of the fallen angels is not accepted in Islamic theology. The offence committed by Satan, according to the Holy Bible is "treason" — wanting to exalt himself to equality with God. Satan says:

"...I will ascend into heaven, I will exalt my throne above the stars of God: I will sit also upon the mount of the congregation, in the sides of the north: I will ascend above the heights of the clouds; *I will be like the most High*" (Isaiah 14:13,14 KJV).

As it is believed in Christianity, Qur'an also teaches that Satan excites enmity and hatred. He deceives, suggests vanity and that he is an evil spirit, rejected, accursed and should be treated as an enemy. (See Fatir, verse 6.)

"Verily, Satan is an enemy to you: so treat him as an enemy...."

But what is the suggestion for the *"treatment"*? The weapons used in fighting the evil spirit (Satan) are stones. Every year, during the fulfillment of one of the five pillars of Islam; i.e., the *Hajj* all the pilgrims to Saudi Arabia on that holy pilgrimage would gather seven stones to throw at Satan. Each pilgrim throws his stones at Satan, after some ritualistic exercises including kissing of the black stone built into a wall. This symbolizes concentration in the love of Allah.

Sin/Righteousness

Islamic theology believes in the concept of evil and good. The evil deeds are the sinful acts, while the good works are the righteous acts. However, the concepts of sin and righteousness in Islam are not the same as in Christianity. The whole thing is like the theory of culture, which says every culture is supreme within its own context.

Ayatollah Khomeni said, "The purest joy in Islam is to kill and be killed for Allah..." because these acts are regarded as *sunnah* in Islamic theology. That is to say that the practices are excellent or legitimate and acceptable acts. However, a convert in Christianity, such as Saul (Paul), must repent of such acts because they are not *"Sunnah"* in Christianity; they are punishable by God.

In Islam, there are degrees and classifications of sins. There are "big" sins and "small" ones. Qur'an teaches that anyone who runs away from the great sins may be taken to paradise (Sura 53:31-32). Allah also says, "If ye (but) eschew the most heinous of the things which ye are forbidden to do, we shall expel out of you all the evil in you, and admit you to a gate of great honors (Sura 4:31).

The solid meaning of righteousness in Islam is *good works*. Allah promises he may reward those who do good with goodness and those who keep aloof from *the great sins* and the indecencies. But the simple sins he will liberally forgive (Sura 53:31b-32). It may be difficult for a Pentecostal Charismatic to accept this, knowing that the Bible says, "*All* unrighteousness is sin." A disciple of Jesus even questioned one day, "If this be so, who then shall be saved?" It is only then the meaning of grace in Ephesians 2:8,9 becomes comprehensible. True salvation must be a free gift of a righteous God to the undeserving, helpless man.

Marriage

Marriage is an *obligatory* institution in Islamic theology. Even those who evade the responsibility of raising a family because of financial incapability have their flimsy excuse disposed from a statement of Allah in Sura 24:32b. It states, "...if they are needy, Allah will make them free from want out of his grace...." It is illegal and against Allah's injunction to take a vow of celibacy in Islam, because it is never ordained by Allah.

However, even though it is not an ordinance in Christianity, God recognizes people who *willingly* accept celibacy for the sake of the Kingdom.

In Islam, Allah allows polygamy (see Sura 4:4). A Muslim is free to marry up to four wives and even more. For the ones who may not be able to pay dowry, Allah permits them to "possess" slave girls of their choice. Even for this, there is no problem theologically according to Sura 4:3,25. By this, Allah recognizes slave ownership and treatment. If a troop of Muslims invades a city, it is an opportunity for the jihadists to get free wives and slaves. To Allah this is acceptable.

Islam is not exclusive when it comes to social inter-course (marriage inclusive) with the Christians. A Muslim woman may not marry a non-Muslim man, because she would lose her Islamic status for that of the non-Muslim husband. But Christian girls are encouraged to be married to Muslim men, knowing that she automatically loses her Christian status, because she would be expected to accept Islam eventually. Qur'an says in Sura 5:6 *that lawful unto the Muslims in marriage are (not only) chaste women who are Muslims, but also chaste women among the Christians.*

Many Moslem boys seek to impregnate Christian girls, because of special prizes promised Muslim youths who impregnate a certain number of girls in Nigeria. Any lady impregnated in that exercise would become a Muslim. Otherwise, she loses her *pride* and some important social status in the African moral society. In Christianity, marriage with unbelievers is not allowed. Ephraim, Samson and some Israelites suffered for this unholy alliance, which is called *unequal yoking.*

For the Muslims, they are still promised some incred-ible number of virgin ladies and concubines to satisfy their sexual urges, even in heaven.

Heaven and Hell

Islam teaches that there will be judgment and punish-ment for those who would not believe and do good works, including those who will fail to believe in Jesus Christ. In Sura 3:54-56, it says:

> *When Allah said: "O Jesus! I will cause you to die and exalt you in my presence and clear you of those who disbelieve and make those who follow you above those who disbelieve to the day of resurrection; then to me shall be your return so I will decide between you concerning that which you differed. Then as to those who disbelieve, I will chastise them with severe chastisement in this world and the hereafter, and they shall have no helpers."*

Hell is synonymous with fire in Islam. It's a place of crying, torment, loneliness, suffering and deep bitterness and of boiling water. But the punishment in hell fire, according to Islamic theology, is not eternal (Sura 6:129; 11:107). Allah could do as he pleases. The doctrinal clause is, "Except as Allah is pleased," and there shall be deliverance after all.

However, in heaven, it is an everlasting enjoyment: Living in some mansions drinking wine and fruit juice. Marrying and having *fun* with beautiful girls. They would exclaim. "O! This is the kind of fruit we used to eat," because Allah promises them "the like" (Sura 2:25b). Imagine that in the Muslim heaven, someone would exclaim at your dining table, "O Tom Blue, this is the apple grown and eaten at Mississippi, the very like of it."

In the Christian heaven, there shall be no marriage, for there shall be no sex. The Bible says we shall be like the angels. Anyone who wants to enjoy fruit salad and sex twenty-four hours a day had better chose Islam. It's just unfortunate that I will not be in the Muslim heaven! I would want to know how Allah handles the case of Mohammed taking his adopted son's wife, Zainab, and reciting, "Praise belongs to Allah, who turned his (Mohammed's) heart toward another man's wife, claiming it was divine, and not lustful and wicked desires.

I'm sure some American cowboys would go to that kind of paradise with their guns to shoot Allah on his throne if he (in his justice) would justify Mohammed for taking their wives in the name of *Sunnah*.

Also, the Qur'an teaches that there is no sure guarantee for going to heaven only because Allah can mislead whom he wishes to mislead and save whom he wishes.

In fact, *all Muslims would go to hell*, while some would be delivered later and the evildoers be left in the fire (Sura 19:71-72).

Therefore, every Muslim is a candidate of hell-fire, whether they like it or not. Allah has fixed it so!

How could Allah do that? Could that be a just God, most merciful, most compassionate? Look at chapter 19 from verse 68 downward. I had to consult several Qur'ans, and all the translations I consulted communicated the same idea. Could Mohammed have made a mistake? Actually, I felt like Joseph Hall (a preacher in the reign of James I), who characterized Mohammed as "that cozening Arabian whose religion, if it deserves that name, stands upon nothing but rude ignorance and palpable imposture...a subtle devil in a gross religion...a monster of many seeds, and all accursed." And to be frank, all are accursed in deed, for their Qur'an to say "... this is an unavoidable decree of your Lord."

> Romans 8:1 KJV says, *"There is therefore now no condemnation to them which are in Christ Jesus...."* This is what the Christian Bible teaches. Isaiah 1:18 KJV says, *"Come now, and let us reason together, saith the Lord: though your sins be as scarlet, they shall be as white as snow; though they be red like crimson, they shall be as wool."*

It says those who believe in Christ have passed from death unto life (1 John 3:14). It also says the *Christian believers* have been called out of darkness into God's marvelous light, while the *Muslim believers* have been *"unavoidably"* decreed to go to hellfire, a place of sorrow, bitterness, darkness and gnashing of teeth. If I knew Allah's address, (this Allah is not the same with God Almighty — see chapter 3), I would counsel with him to stop using Islam as a seed of slavery against humanity. If he could lose the grip of Islam on me, he must on Saudi Arabia, Indonesia, Africa and even the United States. Praise God!

Angels

The existence of angels is important to Islamic teaching. Gabriel, the leading angel, appeared to Mohammed and was instrumental in delivering the revelation in the Qur'an to Mohammed. Al-shaytan is the devil and most likely a fallen angel or jinn. Jinns are those creatures between angels and men which can be either good or evil. Each man or woman has two recording angels — one who records the good deeds, the other who records his bad deeds.

Scriptures

There are four inspired books in the Islamic faith. They are the Torah of Moses, the Psalms (Zabur) of David, the Gospel of Jesus (the injil) and the Qur'an. Muslims believe that the former three books have been corrupted by the Jews and the Christians.

3
The god of Islam

Why do some Muslims call **Allah** instead of *God* while making statements in English? Why do I hear things like "May the Almighty **Allah** bless you"? Why not, "May the Almighty God bless you"?

If I can say in Arabic, "Allau akbar," why can't I say in English, "Praise God," without prejudice or confusion on whom I am praising? Why do I say, "Praise Allah"?

I was playing in the neighborhood among other children as a child, and somebody asked, "Who is God's child?" All the children around raised their hands. My teacher overheard this and immediately he called me in, pulled my ears and said, "You are not God's child; you are His slave," and then quoted Qur'an (chapter 112), which says God was not begotten and He begot no one.

At school, on the contrary, other Christian children would recite John 3:16, and I argued with them that God had no Son (the result of my indoctrination).

Eventually, I found that to the Christians, the sonship of Jesus was symbolic of faith and the key to salvation, while to the Muslims, the sonship of Jesus was an abomination of an infidel.

I had never seen God nor Allah, but I began to evaluate their attributes through the testimonies of the followers — the Christians and the Muslims.

Our exploration on this subject is not necessarily about the contrast, evaluation, or elevation of some subjective whimsies in favor of our religions or politics. Of course, until

41

the end of the universe, there shall be the existence of a followership of Jehovah, Allah, atheism and of other gods of mythology.

But Who Is This Same Allah?

Yes, I read in the Quran of his wonderful deeds: He lowered the holy book from heaven to his chosen prophet, Mohammed (Sura 53:4). Mohammed never wrote a letter. Everything was absolutely the revelation of the Almighty Allah. (That is the claim, so let's be tolerant, at least for now.) The Qur'an was not a by-product of any philosopher's thought, so the non-Muslims need a pretty good measure of tolerance to appreciate the bedrock of this religion. For the root of it rests solely on this prime foundation of Islamic theories, faith, beliefs, values and practices, whether realistic, esoteric or ultra mundane.

The majority of the whole world believes that there was creation with a Master-Mind behind it: He is called the most Supreme Being. His revelation to mankind and His deeds among men accrued Him other qualifying attributes which also stand for His names today. To the Moslems, this most supreme being is called Allah. And technically, none is qualified to describe him or evaluate his attributes, because he is beyond description. But could he be the same God who said, *"This is my beloved Son, in whom I am well pleased"* (Matthew 3:17 KJV) and still offered in chapter 112 of the Quran?

Because of the unmistaken loyalty, commitment and the absolute devotion of certain Christian and Muslim devotees, I want to assume that something is wrong with the perception of one religious sect about the Almighty. Otherwise, the Almighty probably had double masks, portraying His dual characters to the two camps.

Because of this confusion, let's look into the Bible, the Quran and the Hadith for a balanced study.

God's Name in Islam

To identify or recognize any person, place, or thing, a name is desired. Even when Moses encountered God, he asked Him who He was and God responded, *"I AM THAT I AM"* (Exodus 3:14 KJV). In Islam, God's identity is recognized by nomenclature. Islam never existed until about 600 years after Christ. People who lived then were forced to appreciate a new way of life, culture, values and religion, accompanied with a divinely sent manuscript to uphold the new values and divine precepts. If religion, according to the definition by *Oxford Advanced Learners' Dictionary*, is something that one considers oneself *bound* to do, I do not blame the people of Mecca for probing the Islam of Mohammed in the light of the sender; i.e., Allah, during his early evangelism.

Hence, the prophet of Islam himself introduced this personality called Allah. Little did Mohammed know that Allah existed among Arabs as a name given to a god. Just as Africans make names out of statements, it is similar among the Jews and the Arabs. The name *Allah* is the short form of *al-el-hu*, meaning the one who is strong and almighty. The Arabs had other gods who stood as mediators between them and Allah, and their supreme idol god was also called Allah, with the above meaning. But Mohammed introduced the Allah that needed no mediator. He exists alone as single. Therefore, the Trinity doctrine of the first century was different from the injunction of the Allah that Mohammed introduced. To the Arabs generally, Allah is one of the oldest names of a god in their nation.

In the Qur'an, Allah has up to 550 names, as discovered and published by some Islamic scholars in the recent times. Some of them are actually imperative, but in Sura 7:179;17:110 20:8;59:23-24, we find references regarding the excellent names of Allah. The Muslims are advised, in tradition, to recite the ninety-nine excellent names of Allah, and anyone who does that will go to heaven. I also learned to recite some of them when I was in Arabic school. The most popular of these names are:

Al-Rahmam	- The Merciful
Al-Rahim	- The Compassionate
Al-Alim	- The Omniscient

Without any doubt, all these are well recognized attributes of Almighty God.

His Natural Characteristics

1. He is the Creator
2. He is eternal
3. He is glorious
4. He is unchangeable
5. He is invisible
6. He is infinite
7. He is omnipresent
8. He is omnipotent
9. He is perfect
10. He is unexplainable and inexplicable
11. He is incomparable

His Moral Character

1. He is pure
2. He is just; i.e., equitable
3. He is merciful
4. He is compassionate

All these and more describe the qualities of Allah, based upon the revelation received by Mohammed. Allah's natural qualities are similar to the testimonies the Christians share about their God, the Father of our Lord Jesus Christ.

But what's the difference, if there is any, between this Allah of Islam and the God Christians proclaim?

Holiness

There is an uncompromising demand for purity among Muslims, just as the holy God in Christianity makes it a command for Christians. In fact, in Islam, there is a special bath one must take before worshipping Allah if he has just finished having sex with his spouse. And before any worship service, a worshipper who has previously eaten and drunk must make some ritual before his prayer, called Salat. This is an ablution which demands the washing of hands, mouth, nose, face, arms, head, ears and feet before the prayer or worship is acceptable.

But in Christianity, the purity God demands is an inward type, the Spirit type, the heart-motivated worship or prayer. Both the Old and New Testaments of the Bible reveal that sin, purity and impurity are the things of the heart and not of the body, even if the body is used to execute the acts of holiness or impurity (Matthew 23:26).

Fatherhood

In Islam, Allah reveals himself as the creator and the only one. He is the same distant, mighty judge before whom every creature must tremble. "Fatherhood" is not in his personality (Sura 5:18). His followers are regarded as slaves rather than children.

On the contrary, God in Christianity from the Old Testament through the New, has kept a "fatherhood" relationship with Adam, angels and the New Testament believers. He, as opposed to Allah of Mohammed, communes with man and has fellowship with him as a Father.

Even to the Christians, the fatherhood of God is a mystery, and it is privileged (1 John 3:1). All these distinguishing features of two elements are leading us somewhere.

Omni Qualities

In Islam, Allah is omniscient and omnipotent. That means he does not deserve the service of any media house to know what goes on in different countries at different times.

He also has the natural ability to be everywhere at all times simultaneously. He revealed himself to Mohammed as omnipotent; i.e., he possesses unlimited power. Therefore, he does not need any military attaché to be his bodyguard. Unfortunately, in the midst of trouble, challenge and defilement of his Islamic injunction, his omnipotent quality is too weak to contend with his enemies. He would need the service of his followers to threaten, harass and kill his enemies (Sura 47:4).

The true Muslims and the prophets of Allah recognize his limitations in contending with his enemies, so they must resort to helping him.

On the contrary, it is an abomination to help the God of Christianity. In fact, it attracted a death penalty to Uzzah (2 Samuel 6:1-11), who was moved out of compassion and conceived the helplessness of God's ark, but God eventually proved to the people of Israel that He alone can avenge His enemies, protect His integrity and avenge the enemies of His followers. You cannot help the God of Christians, as it is tantamount to disclaiming His omnipotent quality. Hence, as opposed to Allah of Islam, the God of Christianity does not need or permit anyone to take vengeance on His behalf.

Relationship With Jesus

Qur'an teaches that Jesus (Isa) was one the prophets of Allah. Isa was disregarded as the Son of God, but as one of the prophets Who wrought the most miraculous deeds in His time. My teacher taught me as a child to acknowledge Jesus (Isa) as a prophet of God and that God has no child. In Islam, it is ridiculous for God to conceive. In fact, the Muslims appreciate the fact that Jesus was born through the enablement of the Holy Spirit.

To the Allah whom prophet Mohammed represented, Jesus was not a Son. Jesus was just a glorified prophet and teacher. To Allah, according to Mohammed's Quran, Jesus (Isa) was only the Son of Mary (Sura 4:171). Jesus never had any relationship with Him in the Godhead, nor is the issue of Trinity of any significance. I agree that indeed, Allah of Mohammed is not the father of Jesus, nor is the Holy Quran His direct, unintercepted, unmutilated and divine inspiration. If indeed Allah disclaims Jesus as a begotten Son, we had better believe the firsthand information about their relationship. So when Jesus talked about His Father, He was not referring to Allah that Mohammed later manufactured. Therefore, the God of the Bible is not the Allah of the Qur'an. So it can be understood when Moslems disbelieve Christ's sonship.

However, the God of the Christian world declared Jesus as *His begotten Son, in whom He was well pleased* and recommended the whole world to hear Him (Jesus). Could it have been the same God Who spoke these words by His Holy Spirit at the transfiguration that eventually changed His mind 600 years later about His divine relationship with His Son? God forbid. Mohammed misunderstood the sonship of Christ in the hope to become a new champion. In his effort to make his case for his desired position, to give himself some credibility, he propounded the theory that Allah threw down the Quran from heaven. I find it difficult to believe that a book was thrown down from heaven. But I find it easier to believe that the God Who made man and gives him children, begat a Son for Himself.

Emotion

Allah, like any individual, has the ability to hate or appreciate. One of his ninety-nine excellent names in the Quran is Al-Rahman, which means "the merciful." Al-Rahim (the compassionate) proves that he has that tendency in his emotional attributes. Nevertheless, the compassion or judgment of Allah may not necessarily be retributive, because Allah has the veto power to forgive whom he wishes to and condemn whoever he feels like condemning.

This is the reason no Muslim in this world can ever be sure of going to heaven, but must continue to plead for mercy, *even after death.*

But what am I trying to x-ray? The Allah of Mohammed instructs Muslims to attack infidels (i.e., non-Muslims) until they have been killed or wounded (Sura 47:4).

In Matthew 5:17, Jesus said He came to fulfil the law. And that is the reason His precepts were revolutionary to the wicked nature of man. Jesus, the prophet of Allah as "they" claim, teaches His followers to love their enemies and pray for those who persecute them. Can you imagine, to love your enemies? In Luke 6:35-36, He says when you do that, you are manifesting the nature of your Father. No wonder it is almost impossible for Muslims to be called sons of God, because they are instructed to hate and kill their enemies. Allah has a different view for dealing with enemies than Almighty God. In Matthew 5:44, Luke 6:27 and 1 Thessalonians 5:15, Christians are taught never to retaliate. Jesus would not teach His followers to strike the neck of infidels (as Allah instructs in Sura 47:4) because He (Jesus) recognizes that infidels would remain infidels until God Himself, by His divine power, draws them (see John 6:44).

We cannot prove ignorance of the Crusaders' actions between the eleventh and thirteenth centuries when they violently stood to claim Jerusalem from the Islamic and Turkish communities.

Being led of the Spirit of God cannot be misunderstood. Even though the Crusaders used the cross as their symbol, God was not in the battles. They used Christianity as a cloak for violence. Besides, those aggressors were led by the Roman emperors, so the battles can be well appreciated as political wars and not as religious jihad or violence. Whatever the trademark the violence is given, it is obviously contrary to the nature and the teachings of Jesus Christ. As a matter of fact, since the Crusaders' wars, the cross was never again used by anyone to fight any war against Moslems or any other group of people.

While a Muslim receives rewards of Allah for killing an infidel, a Christian awaits reproof for contradicting the nature and the Word of God as written "that the God of

Christians does not delight in the death of an infidel, but that he should come to repentance." (See Ezekiel 18:23,32; 33:11.) Could the Allah of Mohammed be the same with the Father of Jesus and the God of the Christians? Could the same God say, "Kill the infidels" to the Moslem and then turn around and say to the Christians, "I hate the death of the infidel"? One is blood-thirsty; the other is loving and most merciful. The Almighty God of the Christians is obviously *Al-Raham*.

In fact, when some unbelieving messengers came to arrest Jesus, a disciple of Jesus cut off someone's ear, and Jesus was sore disappointed (Matthew 26:51-52).

Now, if Jesus is promoting the will and counsel of Allah and the same Allah teaches Mohammed to disclaim Jesus, *then there must be several Allahs*: That of Mohammed's followers, and that of the Arab Christians and the Hausa Christians in Nigeria. They cannot be the same. They differ in emotion in spite of coincidence of name. In fact, in Northern Nigeria today, some Hausa Christians are selective in the use of Allah because of this anomaly. Some have resorted to using other names for God in Hausa; e.g., Ubangiji. Quran Sura 3:31 says emphatically that "Allah does not love the unbelievers," while John 3:16 says, *"For God so loved the* [unbelieving] *world...."*

If indeed all Scriptures are given by the inspiration of the Holy Spirit and the Quran is also direct revelation from Allah to Mohammed, then there is a glaring conflict of personalities and manifestos.

One thing is very clear. Allah of Mohammed is a spirit, guilty of impersonation, by taking on the name of God deceitfully in order to mislead the world. Of course, we aren't surprised that prophesies are coming to pass. In Nigeria, we have had some Jesuses claiming deity, yet nothing can be truer than the truth. Jesus is the same yesterday, today and forever (Hebrews 13:8). And His relationship with the Father God still remains that of the only begotten Son, *not born of the will of man, but of God*. Praise God.

The traditional concept of the "idol," merciless, almighty Allah of the pre-Islamic Arabs, was carried into Islam by Mohammed. No wonder he is so unmerciful to the infidel. Since he is an idol, he has no heart to feel. It is only the wicked who love those who love them or hate those outside their fold. It is believed that Mohammed transferred the idol of the almighty Allah of the pre-Islamic Arabs to the Ka'bah, which is the content of the dome at the pilgrimage site's central focus, where pilgrims go to kiss when they go to Mecca for the performance of all pilgrimages.

4
Islam and African Slavery

As late as 1993, the subject of slavery in Africa was being revisited by a powerful lobby group urging Nigerians and the government to prevail on the West, especially America and Britain, to make reparations for the havoc the Trans-Atlantic slave trade had wrought on Africa. A leading politician and Islamic leader, Chief M. K. O. Abiola, with the tacit backing of the northern rulers was the arch-apostle of the reparation campaigns. Huge amounts of money were being demanded for damages. Preparations were being made to take the battle to the United Nation's Court at the Hague, Netherlands. However, the annulment of the June 12 elections in Nigeria in 1993 dealt a big blow to the campaign because Chief M.K.O. Abiola was caught up in the web of Nigeria's political intrigues.

Half-truths and outright lies were peddled as the whole truth. The sentiments of people were whipped up in order to generate hatred for the West. America and Britain have been accused of decimating the populations of Africa through the evil of slave trade, that the most productive segment of fit and able-bodied Africans were carried away to power Western farms and industries and that the present economic and social problems facing Africa had their roots in the Trans-Atlantic Slave Trade. The early white missionaries have been labeled as collaborators in this hideous practice.

Reparation calls are economic. This is on the African front. However, the Islamic agenda of becoming a world power of the future must be fought especially on the Western front. That campaign is of a religious nature. Billions of petro-dollars suddenly became available to Arab kings and sheikhs as of October 17, 1973, during the Yom Kippur war against Israel. But for the mercy of God, the rest of Africa would have been overrun by Islam as it happened to the strong Christian community of northern Africa during the Islamic invasion of 632 to 732 A.D. Islam is no longer just closing in on Europe and the United States of America, but the people are being effectively disarmed. Western Christians must be careful not to be caught up in the web of Islam. Subtle methods are being used at the moment. People are taught or instructed to hate. When one is taught to hate, no matter how justified the reason may be, it is always counter-productive. To hate is to nurture ill health for one's self. Hatred plays strange tricks with the memory. It exaggerates injustice and injuries and militates against time's healing touch. "It curdles the milk of human kindness and stunts the development of the soul."

Islam is being promoted as a "brotherhood" religion where equality and eleganitarianism are its hallmarks. In America it is being presented as a religion of Africa. The American Africans are where they are today (in a strange land) because of the evil of slave trade. I condemn slavery in all its forms, except the yoke of Jesus Christ which I willingly and happily carry. The calls and carrots being dangled to American Africans to embrace Islam is jaundiced and is based on the premise of *hate, misinformation* and *lies*. The whole truth needs to be told.

There is a conspiracy to focus only on the evil of the Trans-Atlantic Slave Trade as if it is that easy to re-write the history of Africa. As late as the 1810s and 1820s and in various ways throughout that century, people of my geo-political area had to resist with their blood the encroachments on their lands and the claims of suzerainty in the form of taxes, tributes and slaves.[2] Who were these overlords? Who were those who had to be resisted? Where did they take their slaves? The answers to such questions are open secrets. The slave mongers were the Muslim emirs or kings of Northern Nigeria and elsewhere in sub-Saharan Africa. They did not have the technology or knowledge to be able to take their items of trade to the coasts of Nigeria. Centuries before Europeans "discovered" the dark continent, the Trans-Saharan trade was thriving, especially in slave trading. The continent was also thriving in Islam. If the Trans-Atlantic Slave Trade decimated the coastal peoples of West Africa of their productive population, the Trans-Saharan Slave Trade not only pushed the people of the hinterlands to marginal unproductive lands and hill enclaves, but literally "milliocimated" their populations. Dr. Jan H. Boer in his "Christianity and Islam Under Colonialism in Northern Nigeria" has this to say, and I quote him extensively.

There is one area in which the colonial government definitely suppressed Muslim aspiration and practices in Northern Nigeria. I refer to the practice of wholescale slave raiding and slave trading on the part of the northern Muslims vis-a-vis their traditional neighbors. In the minds of most people, the Trans-Atlantic Slave Trade between West Africans and Europeans stands out more vividly. There was also the large-scale internal trade of Nigerians by Nigerians, traditionalists by Muslims. Without seeking to belittle the Trans-Atlantic trade by contrasting it with the Muslim equivalent, proper historical perspective demands that the latter be examined with the same intensity as the former. As many think they can see a connection between the Trans-Atlantic Slave Trade and the present relationships between Africa and the West, so there are good reasons to posit connections between the Muslim enslavement of traditionalists during pre-colonial days and present concepts of jihad...It is also of historical value to mention some differences between the two slave systems. First, it cannot be denied that there was connivance between Africans and Westerners who came to our shores. The Muslim slave trade was conducted within Nigeria solely by African Muslims. No outside party can be held responsible for it.

Secondly, whereas the descendants of the victims of the Trans-Atlantic trade survived and are easily identified as significant minorities in some countries of the Western hemisphere and as minorities in some countries of the Western hemisphere and as majorities in others, Rev. Dr. Yusufu Turaki, the (former) General Secretary of the Evangelical Churches of West Africa (ECWA) has recently raised the question as to the whereabouts of the offspring of the victims of the Muslim slave trade that were taken to Muslim countries beyond the Saharan desert. Though eyewitnesses insist that the Muslim trade was very extensive, the offspring of the multitude of these slaves are very few in number. They form a mere smattering in the Arab world. "What," demands Turaki, "happened to them?" It is more than a rhetorical question.

Thirdly, without belittling the guilt of so-called Christians involved in Trans-Atlantic slavery, it is a historical fact that it was a combination of economic developments and Christian conscience that forced its abolition. The internal Muslim slave trade was stopped by a combination of Christian and colonial forces. There were no indications that Muslims would have stopped the practice if they had not been stopped by these external non-Muslim forces. In fact, the Qur'an allowed the wholesale trading of slaves.

In the next few paragraphs I want to describe this Muslim slave trade in all its horror. Boer's subsequent paragraphs are indeed like a horror movie and can only be summarized here. Should anyone wish to dismiss Boer's treaties as being from a white missionary,[3] I will show that up to the present time, there are surviving evidences that indeed Islam is the seed of slavery in Africa. Boer gave accounts of emirs sending slave raiders into their territories to collect the annual tribute due them, and in the process destroying, killing, enslaving and utterly devastating large areas as a result of which huge walled towns were deserted.

These people only survived because of the mercy of God and the hill sanctuaries the Muslim horses could not reach.

With prolonged experience of centuries before the Trans-Atlantic Slave Trade was conceived, the cruel and ingenious methods of torturing our people by Muslim slavers became increasingly "refined." The side-effects of this terrorism and cruelty were astounding. For instance, Boer wrote of the Sara-Kabba people who had their women stretch their lower lips to incredible ugliness, not because the men folk thought this beautiful, but to the contrary, supposedly to make them unattractive to Muslim slavers. After centuries of harassment, these people withdrew into swamps. As soon as a stranger came in sight, shrieks, a rush, a rustling in the grass was heard and there would be silence. The population in the village had decamped. Boer finally talked of a veteran missionary's humble hesitation to outrightly support Martin Luther's evaluation of Mohammed as "the firstborn son of Satan" because of Islam's avowed acceptance, practice and teaching of slavery.[4] "The veteran simply did not tire from describing the worst and most flagrant degradation he had witnessed in Africa because of Islam. Muslims were worse than traditionalists in his mind. The darkness of Africa was largely caused by the Muslim slavers. Traditionalists were mostly innocent victims. The Muslims were the perpetrators of Africa's greatest evil, the agents of demonizing Africa. Though he attributed a higher degree of civilization to Islam, they also were regarded as excelling in works of evil. Religious intolerance, brutality, fanaticism, unbridled covetousness, lying and deception were all characteristics of Muslims. Where Mohammedanism (i.e., Islam) has gone, lying, stealing and sexual diseases have spread.

There are several issues of theoretical interest we have raised which cannot be pursued here. However, let me give direct answers to some of the questions Dr. Turaki, a Nigerian as myself, and several other well-meaning people have asked of the whereabouts of our brothers who were taken from Ghana, Mali, Togo, Benin, Niger, Nigeria,

Cameroon, Sudan, Zaire, Kenya, Uganda, Congo, Chad, Central Africa Republic and so on to the Arab world.

We request our brothers in America and in other places of Diaspora to ask the same question. Where are they? And why should reparations not to be made by Arabs to us because of them? One of the saddest commentaries on the dehumanizing effect of the Muslim slave trade, which has never been told anywhere, is the brutal and wicked method by which our brothers were rendered reproductively unproductive. The slaves kept in the palaces of emirs in Africa or taken to the Arab world were denied the power of procreation through systematic and complete castration. This inhuman "treatment" made them fit to serve the emirs and nobles at home and in the Arab world. The singular aim was to ensure that there would be no mixing of blue blood with ordinary blood, the underdogs. That explains how there is only a "smattering" of the black race in the Arab world. Officially today, there are no slaves, but according to the Islamic classification of peoples, there are bonafide slaves whether the Aryan race likes it or not.

Another living witness of the widespread nature of the Muslim slave trade in Nigeria is preserved in the name of the town of Bauchi which will occur in several places in this book. *Bauchi* is the Muslim word for the slave belt outlaying the Hausaland of Nigeria. The term describes the people and the whole area south of the Muslim emirates of Northern Nigeria pre-dating the coming of the British in 1903. Area slaves could be harvested for the market. Slaves from this area and elsewhere served the wives of the emirs and the harem of concubines. Some of them were abused by noble homosexuals. The most intriguing aspect of this Islam brutality is that all the slaves would be initiated into Islam, and yet the promise of "brotherhood" was a mirage to them. The question is, what spirit can permit a member of the brotherhood to be unpersoned to the level of a eunuch except the spirit of evil? A majority of the "Bauchi" slaves entered the Trans-Saharan trade in exchange for slates, trinkets and other articles of trade found in North Africa and Arabia where they became drawers of water and hewers of wood, in addition to satisfying the sexual passions of Muslim homosexuals. They also became the jesters in palaces. Unlike the gold trade between the Arabs and the powerful West African Empires of Ghana, Songhai and Mali, slaves were the commodities of Nigeria.[5]

A third aspect of Muslim slave trading which we must consider has to do with the spread of Islam. This ugly trade was carried through the system of flag-bearing by Muslim chieftains from Africa who went to Mecca on a holy pilgrimage. They would return from Arabia with a flag and a mandate to plant Islam in their domain through the jihad (i.e., holy war). The powers in Arabia would not be satisfied by just a report that the jihad had been successful, but they would instruct them to bring along slaves as tributes, booties, or trophies. If the Trans-Atlantic Slave Trade was bad, the Trans-Saharan was worse. Their slaves were dehumanized through mutilations in the name of circumcision and castration. They were never assimilated into the host community.

A Muslim would have a clear conscience to carry out the slave trade because of the institutionalized categorization of humans by Islam. It serves as an excellent opium to his sick conscience. A human is either born a Muslim dar-al-Islam: "Of the house of Islam/peace," or a dar-al-dhimmi: "Of the house of the protected," or a dar-al-harb: "Of the house of war." No member of dar-al-Islam may be a slave, but we have noted the contradiction with regard to the African slaves. A member of dar-al-dhimmi, which are the so-called people of the book; i.e., Jews and Christians, can only escape slavery on meeting the strict conditionality of being indifferent and non-resistant to activities of the propagation of Islam. There is, of course, no escape for any member of the dar-al-harb, because war must be waged against him. He must be captured and enslaved. This law is secretly still in operation among the Moslems. Any member of dar-al-dhimmi is potentially a member dar-al-harb. A member captured will be incorporated into the house of Islam, but remains a slave or a servant until today.

The Islamic classification of humans is at the root of all religious violence in Nigeria. Christians who have their places of worship near a mosque, for instance, are candidates for carnage because they have not kept to the condition of sitting a church far away from a mosque.

The final question we may ask in this chapter is, can a member of the house of Islam be a member of the house of war? The testimony of a recent Muslim convert to Christianity will illustrate the point better. Abubakar had a wife and two children until December, 1995. He was a prosperous livestock farmer of a herd of 200 head of cattle, which was passed on to him as the eldest male child. However, today he lives on meager charity from Christians because he lost everything for becoming a member of the house of the protected, a Christian! He escaped being slaughtered in the presence of his wife and children only through God's miracle. He escaped with his family but was found out, and his first child Hamsatu, a four-year-old girl, was kidnapped and taken back to their village. A girl of about the same age was killed last year in a neighboring Fulani camp or village because her father had become a Christian. The murder was to force him give up his faith, but he did not give up and his daughter had to die. In the case of Salihu, the angels had been on assignment on his behalf! He was able to rescue his daughter and today they are living hundreds of miles away from the village.[6]

Many white missionaries and colonial administrators literally died by the hundreds on the soil of Africa in the process of stopping slave trading.

The issue of Islam and slavery is an ever-expanding problem. The slavery, though not obvious, is nonetheless real in the social life of her community. Both women and children suffer in silence under the oppressive decrees of Mohammed in the Qur'an.[7]

5
Islam and Women's Freedom

The position of women in Islam is most unfortunate, and it makes nonsense of the popular slogan of the "brotherhood" of Islam. I will cite authorities on the attitude of Mohammed to women to illustrate their unenviable position. A Muslim man towers like the oaks of Lebanon in comparison to his women folk and is even much taller than non-Muslim men. The Muslim man has absolute authority and rights over the children.

Recently, I went to condole a family in Kano over the death of a friend. He was a very high government official, and his two wives were equally educated in the Western sense. They have both performed the annual pilgrimage to Mecca several times. One month after the passing away of their husband, they have both moved out of his house and left their children behind. The mother of the deceased is now the one taking care of the children. The women have no right of ownership.

The wife of a typical Muslim is not a lifetime companion with equal rights, but is often just a means of satisfying his carnal desires. Muslim men who do not treat their wives in this way are in a very small minority. In Islam the world belongs to men alone. Women must stay in the background. This can be seen in the mosques and other public places. In this regard, the African traditionalist is a hundred light-years ahead of Islam in the humane treatment of women. Islam teaches that a man might have four legal wives at any given time and may choose to keep any number of concubines. That is carried over to even the anticipated life in heaven where a Muslim will have access to hundreds of beautiful women. No wonder the Western fantasies over sex have a wonderful private appeal to Muslim men. What a wretch is a Muslim woman.

According to Islam, Mohammed received a revelation from Allah, through which he learned that any Muslim can legally marry up to four women (Sura 4:3). Muslims can also enter into a temporary marriage. For instance, when traveling, a Muslim man can keep wives in different places or take concubines from among slaves just as it pleases him (Sura 4:3-34). A man may keep himself from his wife as a punishment for disobedience and beat her up (Sura 4:34). The greatest threat to a woman's freedom in Islam is seen best in the Sharia judicial system. The witness of one man at a trial is equal to that of two women (Sura 2:282). That translates into practicality in this manner. If a woman should accuse her husband of adultery and he is able to produce one man to witness in his favor, his wives automatically lose their case. Worse or most repressive still is the fact that a man does not need any formal legal authority to divorce his wife. Should it have been an action carried out in hasty anger, he can remarry her. Later, if he divorces her a second time, he still has the right to remarry her once again. But if he divorces her a third time, he forfeits his legal right to remarry her until she marries another man and has been divorced by him. Then the first man can remarry her (Sura 2:229-230). A wife is regarded as the field of her husband in which he can sow whatever he wishes (Sura 2:223). A wonderful life awaits the faithful Muslim in paradise — trees for shade and fresh fruits, alongside cool rivers, a few dozen maidens and several lads always at his disposal.

Little is said in the Quran about his previous wives in connection with paradise (Sura 55; 56:15-22,72).

Due to the over-dominance of men in Islam, a woman cannot exercise her constitutional and fundamental human rights in the matter of election. The men always tell their Muslim wives how to vote in any general election. This malady is at the root of unfair election results in Nigeria. A non-Muslim party stands very little chance of winning an election in Northern Nigeria because the women are always in seclusion. A good housewife should not be seen in public except for emergencies and even so she must have a veil covering for the head and face, leaving only the eyes opened. During elections they troop out in large numbers to choose candidates who had no access to them during electioneering! Invariably, they all vote according to the dictates of their husbands.

It is not just married women who have no freedom in Islam, but girls of marriage age also. Binta is a recent Muslim convert a member of our team is presently discipling. She accepted Christ in the Junior Secondary School away from her home in Ningi town. She is afraid for dear life to disclose to her parents her new faith. She doesn't stand any chance of living, in case she hurriedly does so. Her father is the spiritual leader in their community. During the summer when she was on vacation, her parents were suspicious when they noticed she was not observing the regular prayer times. She explained she was menstruating. A few days later she was still not praying as expected, and she gave the same excuse. This time her mother had to examine her. Thanks be to God, a miracle took place and within four weeks she had her period twice! In the next episode, her parents told her they would marry her out. She complained that she was still in school, and she was asked to marry a man she did not know. God intervened again, and she ran away to her aunt's place. No Muslim girl has the right to choose her life partner since marriage is not determined by love or affection.

In conclusion, may I now give you the insight on the love life of Mohammed, the father of Islam? You must have reached the conclusion on the basis of the previous accounts that the liberty and freedom women have under Islam cannot be compared to that under Christianity.

According to the "True Guidance, Part One," Mohammed followed his passions. Anas quotes Mohammed as
having said, "I was given excellence in four things more than
any other man: Generosity, courage, intercourse and killing."
Salihu informs us that Mohammed said, "My great love is
prayer, but greater than this is my love for perfume and
women." Mohammed al-Ishmawi says that God gave
Mohammed the following rights, which were not granted
to any other believer.

1. The right to cool shade.

2. The right to bounties.

3. The right to nine wives at once.

4. The right that his wives marry none other than him.

5. The right to marry a woman who offers herself to
   him (Sura 33:44).

6. The right to put away any wife, take any wife, and
   seek again the wife he set aside (Sura 33:51).

7. The right to seize the best of any bounty, be it
   slave man, slave girl, or breastplate, and with or
   without his participation in battle (Sira Halabiyya,
   Vol. s).

8. The right to demand that his son-in-law ask
   permission if he desires to marry other women.

9. The right to look at a woman who was not his wife
   and to be alone with her to prevent him from lust-
   ing (Sira Halabiyya, section on the conquest of Banu
   Salim).

10. The right to have sexual relations during Ihram,
    the pilgrimage (Sira Halabiyya, section on Imral
    al-Qada).[8]

What especially reveals Mohammed's caprice and
inability to restrain himself? His greatest error was when he
married his adopted son's wife. Though his people
reproached him, he paid no heed, for when hurtful desires

dominate the soul, it makes a person irrational. Mohammed, however, claimed that God had commanded him to act as he did; thus, he established his sin as a custom and law for every man.

It is recorded in Sura 33:49, "...And any woman believer, if she gives herself to the Prophet and if the Prophet desire to take her in marriage, for thee exclusively, apart from the believer...." Um Sherik al-Dusiya offered herself to Mohammed. She was beautiful, and he accepted her. Aisha (Mohammed's wife) said, "There is no good in a woman who gives herself freely to a man." Um Sherik answered, "I am that woman." Mohammed then called her a believing woman. When he had said so, Aisha returned, "God is quick to fulfil your desire" (Suyuti's Asbab al - Nuzul on this verse). Aisha was right in her statement that there is no good in a woman who gives herself freely to a man; such a one is depraved. Anyone who approves of her behavior will be like her. The god of Mohammed was quick to approve all that his sinful heart desired. It is recorded. Thou mayest put off whom thou wilt of them, and when thou will thou mayest take to thee and if thou seekest any thou hast put aside, there is no fault in thee..." (Sura 33:51). The meaning of the phrase is that the Lord allowed Mohammed to abandon or to sleep with any of the women, according to his wish. These words are among the indication that the Qur'an is void of divine inspiration. Far be it from God to permit a prophet, the recipient of revelations, to indulge in lust and revel with women at his pleasure. Mohammed embraced those who captured his mind and heart with their beauty, such as Aisha and Zainab, and treated the rest poorly.

The Lord God is neither corrupt nor apprehensive. When holding a feast on the occasion of his wedding to Zainab, Mohammed invited the people and provided them with food. But he desired them to leave, because his mind was occupied with his bride...When he stood up to leave the third time, all the people departed, and Mohammed entered his home. Anas followed him, but Mohammed prevented him by lowering the curtain between them. Thus, we read the following verse in Sura 33:53: "O believer, enter not the houses of the Prophet, except leave is given you...." Is it reasonable that divine revelation should occupy itself with such personal matters as the marriages and wedding ceremonies of Mohammed?

In the same verse, we find reference to what Talha, the cousin of Aisha, had done. Mohammed saw him talking with Aisha, so he said to him, "Do not claim this status from now on." Talha answered, "She is my cousin, and my God, neither I nor she has said anything shameful." Mohammed said, "There is nobody who is more jealous than God, and there is nobody who is more jealous than I." Talha left saying, "When Mohammed dies, I will surely marry Aisha after him." Thus the Koran says, "It is not for you to hurt God's messenger, neither to marry his wives after him ever...."[9]

The freedom and equality which the Bible, and especially the New Testament, offer Christian women is not comparable to what Islam offers.

As has already been mentioned, Islam was not only an active participant in the slavery of human beings but of the soul of people. Mohammed, from the above example, was unfortunately trapped in the prison of illicit passion. He made no effort to free himself of the cancer because he did not know any better. So is the situation of all Moslems. They are trapped and locked up by sin and all its vices. I see some Moslems genuinely seeking for God and a release from the oppressive forces of their animalistic tendencies or urges. Because they have been bound and blinded by Islam, they cannot see the God-given liberty offered by the releasing and delivering power of the cross of Christ. The power Moslems need to add to their religious energy is the sacrifice of Christ. Nothing in the world has so bound millions of people into the suffocation of sins, problems, sicknesses, diseases and poverty like Islam. But one with rational thinking will wonder how such a religion devoid of the power to transform people into a newness of life can spread so far and wide. The answer is simple and not far-fetched. The Almighty is not in it. Then, I believe the only option one is left with is that of a subtle demon spirit of diversion and hindrance. It must be the force of the lawless one. That is why Moslems are so lawless.

In nations such as Algeria and Egypt, where Islamic revolutionary groups are not the law-makers but are struggling against the forces of democracy to set up their own system of government, Moslems do not keep or obey government laws. Even in Nigeria, for instance, where Islam can never be final authority in government, Moslems do not see themselves as being governed by the laws of the land. When they break any law, they say Allah allowed them to do so. They are a law of their own. They break government laws flagrantly, and anyone who dares to challenge them is placed under serious persecution, unlike Christians who are obedient to the Biblical instruction to obey the government and the laws of the land.

When you look at a typical Moslem, he looks really troubled, harassed, tense, hassled and confused. There is nothing calm about him. Troubles and enmity are no new thing to him. A true Moslem will quickly remind you that he is not afraid of a fight because he was born and bred in it. In spite of all these negative trends, inabilities and shortcomings in Islam and in Moslems, addicts are so tied to serving the religion as slaves, they cannot help but serve their master.

I asked one Moslem rich man who dared to confide in me about his emptiness, lack of peace and guilt, "Why do you keep going to the mosque since this does not help you deal with your shortcomings?" He said it is like he has been bound to it, even though he sees the difference in Christianity. Something seems to be hindering him from making a positive decision for Christ. He is ashamed of the violent tendency of Moslems. He wonders if a true God will permit all the needless killings. He believes his religion needs to be more peaceful and friendly. But the power to make these changes is what Moslems are lacking. This is such a contrast to what the Bible describes as true religion. The Bible says true religion from the Almighty God is first peaceable, appeasable and it transforms (James 3:14-18). True religion possesses the ability to change hearts, and it brings peace, joy and contentment. Islam is a stranger to all of these qualities.

An imam may teach you not to beat your wife, but he will surely go home and beat his wives since the Koran allows him to do so. He has no willpower not to do so. The desire to do good is there, but the willpower to do so is missing. This is the weakness of the flesh. This is the life of the natural man. The thing he really wants to do, he cannot, but the things he does not want to do are the very things he does. In Christ, both the will and power to do good are available. It is only in Christ that you find men who are released to speak and do right honestly, not with eye service.

In Islam the heart is the problem. Moslems struggle to subdue their hearts with laws, rigidity, formalism and constant prayers, but the heart is beyond man. It cannot be understood by man. Nor can it be tamed by a man or religious practices. No matter how often you wash your feet and pray, Jesus said:

> "But when ye pray, use not vain repetitions, as the heathen do: for they think that they shall be heard for their much speaking" (Matthew 6:7 KJV).

Man's religion is always rendered powerless by the changes of the heart which come upon the natural man. But in Christ, the power of God is available both to warn us and to help us check such tendencies. Self-control is not in the dictionary of Moslems. It is a strange word. It is only in Christ that you find self-control personified. Mohammed followed all his animalistic tendencies. In Islam the lawless one has created a counterfeit religious diversion. He filled it with so many legalistic activities to give it some credibility. But salvation is not a result of our works. If it were by works, none of the human race would ever be saved. Islam was fabricated to block people from seeing and receiving the truth of the Gospel. The result is a serious human bondage to all forms of weaknesses and habits. Mohammed never said he came from heaven. He claims to have been spoken to by an angel. Jesus said He came down from heaven. He is the Bread of Life — the way, the truth and the life. He and the Father are one.

Mohammed said his book, the Koran, was thrown down from heaven. But Jesus came from heaven. Who would you choose to believe, a man or a book? Who possesses life, man or a book? Who can physically touch you and free you from all your bondages, a man or a book?

6
Human Bondage

Islam is the ultimate prescription for loose and confused living. It is a disease worse than cancer in its damaging and debilitating effects. When Islam holds sway over a people, they become like empty, hollow trees pretending to be alive but they are very dead. Islam kills and the method by which its hollow ideas are passed on is through rote.

From very early life, innocent children are forced with whips to recite incomprehensible portions of the Qur'an. Most of them grow up not knowing what they are reciting. They just go through life pretending they are Moslems. They are not allowed any chance to critically examine the ideas with which they have been brainwashed. They become zombies whose lives revolve around a lifeless set of ideas that have corrupted their mind and rendered them incapable of free choice in terms of ideas with which they interact. Islam promotes poverty in the area of ideas. Thus, lack of well thought out and tested ideas produce a people who are incorrigible. Each time they are called upon to defend the ideas they hold to, they resort to violence. This is intended to cover up the fact that they have no credible defence for the ideas they hold to. This poverty of ideas reflects in the general populace in various ways. It is among the Moslems that you get the worst record of illiteracy. Most cannot read or write in Arabic and most often even in the first language. This situation results in inadequate communication skills acquisition. This lack of communication skills promotes isolation. They are regrettably isolated from the circuit of the flow of ideas. And when you are isolated from the "flow of ideas," it means other people develop, but you are left behind. That is why most often when you look at them as a group, you tend to imagine a cohesive group. It is only a fluke. You are looking at a people who smell and smack of deep poverty. There is no cohesion. All you are looking at are men ready to inflict damage on others because of their own personal lack of progressive ideas. This lack of progressive ideas affects, to a large extent, the degree of access they have to resources, especially material resources.

The human resource is so depraved. They are greatly defunct in the skills that make for good management of their natural resources, not because there is a death of such ideas, but simply because they are too lazy to acquire such skills.

This tendency to laziness is another unpardonable evidence of the wanton damage that Islam can do to a people or a person. It is generally a religion for lazy people. Everything must be explained by the simplistic and dubious notion that it is the "will of Allah," even when such situations could have been changed. (This notion will be explored in more depth later.) They are therefore necessarily "backward." They abandon and disdain "Western education" in preference to "Islamic education."

I remember when I was very young and in primary school. Often, when I was coming back from school, I would be accosted by children about my age. They would be singing songs to inform me that I was an infidel for going to school. Meanwhile, they were wasting away at home, not even going to so-called Quranic schools. Where such schools are available, they are run by a hungry-looking, illiterate mallam who only uses the children as beggars instead of teaching them the Koran. For a large part of the day, they are sent into town to beg for money or food.

I remember the practice where, when a family finishes any meal, the leftovers that should normally be served to dogs are now handed to these poorly dressed, sick-looking "Almajiris" (disciples). When you subscribe to Islam, you are subscribing to a beggarly life. All your life you are going to be served remnants of everything. The rich are very rich, and the poor are extremely poor. At the end of the day, these children are far from being Islamic scholars. They become wasted, angry and tense people who are looking for any slight opportunity to vent their anger on society.

Whatever little Quranic education they acquire becomes very poisonous and dangerous. They were promised so much, but by the end of the day, they have been effectively enslaved and taken backwards many generations. Any nation or individual who is unfortunate to be held by Islam, has signed out himself and generations after him to a life of nothingness.

If there is any religion that hates the family institution, it is Islam. Islam disdains the "tie" that is supposed to hold the family together. It actively subscribes to polygamy and polyandry. You are allowed to marry at least four women as wives. Instead of this being a prescription for fidelity, it promotes infidelity of the worst order. Men shamefully sleep around with each other's wives. This results in a high prevalence of sexually transmitted diseases and its accompanying nightmares.

Many children to whom they give birth cannot be assisted by the parents to become useful members of society. Children are forced to start fending for themselves early in life. The boys live through life easy prey to all kinds of anti-social groups. The girls are forced into marital life when they should still be basking in the freedom of childhood days. They are deprived of that active and most important stage of life. They grow up without any beautiful memories of childhood to reflect upon. They grow up looking older than their real ages. In some unfortunate cases, the girls are brutally disvirgined by men much older and stronger than they are. Since their reproductive organs are not mature enough for that kind of torture, vital organs are damaged. They are disabled for life with VVF (visco vaginal fistula). They are promptly discarded by such men who go for other fresh targets available for the "picking."

To further dehumanize the women, they are kept in "purdah." This is a practice where women are not allowed to go out and mix with others simply because of the fear of infidelity. Such women are deprived contact with other human beings, which is so vital for the normal function of the human mind. They are deprived of any opportunity to acquire useful economic skills.

They must wait at home for the meager home support stipends the man brings home. When the man becomes tired of her, he can dispense with her by just writing her a note, even on toilet paper, indicating that she has been divorced and that is the end of the unholy alliance they call marriage.

A Moslem chieftain could be very religious, but the reality of transformation remains elusive. Religious observances are taken too seriously with the hope that they will help a soul into the kingdom of heaven. This is no assurance but a hope against hope. No Moslem can speak assuredly from his heart that he knows he is going to heaven no matter the "sadaka" (alms to the poor), or the "Zakka" (tithes) and offerings he gives. He is in bondage to uncertainty, because though a Moslem washes his feet, head, hands, ears and legs five times a day, his inner filth is not removed by such washing. So the heart still remains filthy, corrupt and loose.

If you meet a Moslem man praying and you cross in front of him, as soon as he finishes his prayer, he will start cursing, fussing and pouring insults on you. This is because Islam lacks the power to do an inner working in the lives of its adherents. A man who has just finished praying should be most gentle, kind and sweet, but that is too much to expect from a Moslem.

In Christianity, the God of the Bible expects the heart of man to be thoroughly purged. He does not care too much about washing the outside, but he is concerned about cleansing on the inside. If a man's inside is clean, then only clean things will come out of him, for it is from within that lusts, murders, fornications, adulteries, theft, bitterness, anger, wrath and unbelief come. These things that come from within defile a man and make him unfit for the kingdom of heaven.

If a man is thoroughly religious and knows not how to control his tongue and temper, how shall a visitor know that such a person is a good man? The heart of man cannot be managed in well-doing. For the heart is desperately wicked and deceitful. Who can understand it? Who can handle it in his own power? Positive attitudes will not help control the heart. It takes a radical, surgical operation from a supernatural sacrifice or solution to handle the situation.

This is exactly where Islam falls short. You have a people genuinely yearning to escape from the corruption within them, but the religion lacks the power to help them. Oh yes, they are pious, but it is all superficial externalities of religion. You find a man doing, saying and pushing things he does not want to do. He is seeking for a way out but can't find it because he is bound by a powerless religion.

In the Nigerian experience, a high government official, who is a Moslem, believes that if he steals government money or collects huge bribes of kickbacks before awarding a multimillion dollar contract and gets away with it, Allah willed it to be so. Otherwise, he would have been discovered. And if he is discovered, Allah equally willed it so. With that type of attitude in a nation where Moslems occupy the key leadership positions politically, it can hardly march forward. The economy of such a nation will be continually vandalized, looted and harassed. While the highly placed and well-connected Moslems will get rich, the poor will get extremely poor. And the nation will be strangled to death and starved of vital amenities that should have made life easier.

When you have people of this caliber planning the future of your nation or family, anything goes. Nothing is challenged since it was Allah who allowed it to happen. Why struggle to change his will? The bondage then continues.

7
Islam and Witchcraft

Another pointer to the deceptive nature of the Islamic religious system is that it is deep in witchcraft and idolatry. What has light got to do with darkness? Every Muslim child from a very tender age is taught how to memorize the Quran, to hate Christians, the magical powers of some Quranic verses and the infallibility of Quranic teachers in the matter of interpretation.

In all the Muslim communities in Nigeria, the office of the Moslem scholar is synonymous with that of a medicine man. He is the one who knows the prescription for every sickness, the potion for good luck and the formula for lovemaking.

He has the power to ward off evil spirits and bad luck. He has complete knowledge on how to make one invincible to every missile, be it conventional or hightech. Every Muslim wears or carries one form of talisman or another. Children may have on the average five amulets around their necks as protection against one mishap or another.

A characteristic of every amulet is that it must contain a relevant written verse from the Qur'an in addition to articles, such as pubic hair, human organs, etc. Islam is a mixture of voodoo, witchcraft and a garb of religiosity.

During the Nigerian Civil War of the mid-sixties, a Muslim war general would not give orders to his troops until he had heard from the four Muslim scholars whose services he had engaged throughout the war. On one fateful day, the subordinate of the general advised against the crossing of the Niger bridge, but the Muslim mallams said, "Cross."

The troops were ordered to cross, and midway on the bridge it was blown up by the enemies. The loss of life was extensive.

During the Maitatsine religious crisis of 1983, the followers of the Muslim sect leader, Mahammadu Marwa, believed they were invincible to bullets. When the combined team of soldiers and policemen surrounded their headquarters after there had been reports of ritual killings against the sect, the followers came out against the police with their bows and arrows.

They were not invincible after all, and they died in large numbers with bodies riddled with bullets.

I have used the generic term *witchcraft* in this chapter to refer to any evil practice of the Muslim which has the tacit support of an interpretation of the Qur'an.

A rich man in the Muslim city of Kano, and a successful businessman, sacrifices a human being every Friday before he attends the Jumaat mosque. The blood of the victim is used to water a flower bed by the balcony where alms are given to the beggars who gather every Friday. Some come in order to get food, and these are the most vulnerable. The youngsters are lured to an enclosure to fetch food. The food is brought out, and they scramble to get a portion. One of them is lured to go into a more hidden enclosure for more food. He goes in and does not come out again. There is no way for his friends to find out that he is missing. That sacrifice is to Allah to ensure that the wealth never dries up.

Dele Alabi met Christ when he was an apprentice to his Muslim father, a specialist in Islamic voodoo for his Muslim clients. He reported that before they made every talisman for each of their clients, they would recite some verse of the Qur'an. When the client receives his ware, more incantations not necessarily from the Qur'an, are made to increase its potency. Dele actually met Christ when he had access to an English translation of the Qur'an. Some of the pronouncement on Christ in the Qur'an agreed with what

Christians had been sharing with him. His father also became a Christian two weeks before he met his death. He was unable to move any part of his body for four weeks! However, he conceded to the request of prayer for healing by two Christians.

A fast for twenty-four hours was declared for him, and after the special prayers, his mobility was restored immediately. His condition also improved, and he was able to talk and to make a confession of faith in Christ and to share his testimony.

The testimonies in this short chapter lead us to this conclusion: The spirit who calls himself Allah and claims to have inspired Mohammed, cannot be the Father of our Lord Jesus Christ. Instead, he is a spirit full of lies and violence, who took upon himself the old Arabic name of Allah, wearing it over his face like a mask and claiming to be God, although he is *not* God. Allah in Islam *is an unclean spirit of Satan*, who rules with great power in a religious disguise to this very day (John 8:30-48).

8
Islam — the Violent Spirit

Demonic Prejudice

If you had my type of background and lived all the days of your Christian life in a Moslem-dominated area like I have, you would recognize Muslims as a violent people who are not in any way hesitant to take up the sword against their "infidel" neighbors.

Islam always turns from non-Muslims, even without provocation. Islam impels her adherents to be aggressive for their faith. They are motivated by the spirit of cruelty and a desire to loot and drain the resources of people. They are known to attack, maim and cause suffering, and do not by choice give their homes to tenants of other religions. When they do, with any small fallout, they quickly eject such tenants. A Moslem would not share his house with a person of some other religion. While others can accommodate the Moslem, the Moslem is told not to accommodate people of another belief.

During conflicts, they are known to be merciless. They will kill women, the aged, the sick, children and all who are their opponents. They are known to lock up whole families in their homes and set them ablaze in the house after pouring gasoline all over the place. If you live in a community where almost everyone is a Moslem, or where there are very few Moslems, you may not realize their cruelty until you move to a place where they are a major minority where they are always scheming and plotting wickedness.

In the year 1992, the Chief Imam Gumi of Kaduna, Nigeria, made a statement that he would never live to see a Christian rule Nigeria. The theory of Islam never allows "infidels" to rule over Muslims. And sure enough, in 1993 before General Ibrahim Babangida was going to hand over to an interim government to be led by a Christian, Alhaji Gumi died suddenly. Islam never contemplated the possibility of Muslims living under the rule of "unbelievers."

In their mind, the world is divided into two parts: The one is Dar-al-Islam, the abode of Islam, while the other is Dar-al-harb, the abode of war. The implication is that if Islam is not controlling a society, the society is to be conquered by war. The Quran does not in any way give the "infidel" equal status with the Muslim. The infidel's testimony in the sharia court of justice is not equal with that of a Muslim. The Muslim is always right, but the non-Muslim is not to be trusted. There is no death penalty to a Muslim who kills or does violence to a Christian or to a non-Muslim. But the non-Muslim who kills a Muslim is liable to instant death, even if the non-Muslim is the son of a king or a prince.

In order to justly grasp the significance of Muslim persecution and prejudice, documented evidence will be presented here that will throw further light on the subject.

In the book, *The Fortress and the Fire*, Phil Parshall quotes Merlin Swartz concerning the position of the minorities in Arab lands following the rise of Islam.

> *"Jewish and Christian physicians were not to practice their profession among Muslims. Minority merchants were to pay double the amount of duty for goods they imported. Moreover, the Christians and Jews were not to erect new houses of worship, though they were allowed to keep the old ones in a state of good repair. Perhaps most seriously of all, minorities were required to indicate their identity by wearing special badges or styles of clothing."*

This is still true in countries controlled by fanatical Islamic groups.

Between 1012 and 1014 A.D., it is estimated that some 30,000 churches were destroyed or pillaged in Egypt and Syria. These dates are some eight decades before the first Christian Crusaders.

It is well to bear this in mind when the view is brought that Muslim intolerance is a direct result of attacks of Western Christendom.

In 1670, 15,000 Christian boys, after an Islamic invasion in Crete, were said to have been circumcised in one day, with death the result for most of them. Martyrs were frequently reported in such instances. Beginning with the ninth century, jealousy of Christians in administrative posts was a serious matter, leading to frequent violence and dismissal of non-Muslims.

Muslims find it hard to separate political life from religious life. The introduction of the office of the caliph after the death of Mohammed meant a centralization of governmental powers and religious powers into the office of one man. Both could not be separated.

Dr. Johannes Lepsius gives an interesting insight into the Armenian massacres of 1914-1918 where thousands of Christians were killed. The tie-in between the political and religious aspects of this tragedy are evident.

What are the Armenian massacres then? Without question their origin was political, or to state it more exactly, they were an Islamic administrative measure. But facts prove that, considering the character of the Mohammedan people whose very political passions are roused only by religious motives, this massacre took the form of a religious persecution of a gigantic scale. Are we then simply forbidden to speak of the Armenians as persecuted on account of their religious belief only?

If so, there have not been any religious persecutions in the world. For all such, without exception, have been associated with political movements. Even the death of Christ was a political move which turned the balance at His condemnation.

Moslems would prefer to make any persecution look like a mere political or administrative move, to save the religion from embarrassment. If such persecutions are not religious, why is it that only people of other religions are victims and Moslems are never involved? Such massive killing of Christians is normally carried out in Moslem-dominated areas.

The Moslem turks conquered Greece in the fourteenth century, and then proceeded to heavily tax the Christians in the following manner:

1. *The poll tax.* This was a perpetual tax collected from Christians which provided nearly two-thirds of the revenue of the whole Ottoman Empire.

2. *A 5 percent tax on imports and exports.* If the trader was a Muslim, the rate was halved.

Also for over 300 years, in every fourth year, a fifth of all Christian boys six or nine years of age in Greece were drafted for service in the Turkish military.

There seems to be an almost insidious smothering effect on Christians who seek to let their light shine for Christ within the context of a strictly Muslim society, such as Iraq, Iran, Libya, Syria, etc.

The tie-in between the state and Islam proves to be an insurmountable barrier to overcome. An overt Christian witness in a Muslim-dominated area will be met with fervent, brutal rebuttal and stringent persecution. Soon the Christian comes to feel it is so futile to try converting a Muslim society, so why oppose the Islamic system? The best course of action seems to be no action. So the local indigenous Christian falls into a pattern of not witnessing. This amounts to infringement of the human rights of the Christian (infringement on the freedom of expression).

The Bauchi "Jihad" of Carnage

Bauchi is a city of about 300,000 people and also a capital city of Bauchi state comprising about 60 percent Moslems and 40 percent Christians and others. Moslems make up the bulk of the population in the central part of the town. They also form 70 percent of the ruling class. The governor of the state is a Moslem. The police commissioner of the state is a Moslem. And the commanding officer of the armored unit of the Third Armoured Division is a Moslem. The director of the state security service is a Moslem. The mayor or emir of the city is a fanatical Moslem. The chairman of the Bauchi local government area is a fanatical Moslem.

The stage was set for a total eradication of all "infidels." A series of meetings were being held by the Islamic strategic leaders in preparation for a jihad. Unfortunately, the target groups of Christians and others were unaware of what was about to happen.

Rumors, however, had it that young Moslems were being trained in secret places on the art of the use of guns, swords, daggers, clubs and everything possible that could cause death or grievous bodily harm. Some of the trainees were as young as nine years of age. They were being trained on how to cut off heads, legs, arms and fetuses from pregnant women's abdomens with only one strike. They were being trained night and day. The teachers were seasoned military officers. The training sessions also included the skills of laying an ambush, instant vanishing and regrouping techniques.

A well-trained team of violent people was put together, waiting for the signal to attack and rid the city forever of all "infidels." The jihadists were also armed with petrol gas tanks, machetes, and a list of all the people who must be eradicated — such included all Christian ministers and Christian government officials who had been a problem to their religion or to Moslems.

They were also armed with the maps of all target churches, Christian homes, Christian schools, etc. A backup force was also organized from neighboring states and villages, which included Kaduna and Kano states, Toro and Azare.

It was Saturday, April 20, 1991. The jihadists were in great fury, like the fury that possessed Herod when he went out to destroy the infants at the time of the birth of Christ. They kicked off their cleansing massacre against all non-Muslims by attacking Christians who were gathered together in a church house for a wedding celebration. They were armed with swords, daggers, knives, clubs, gasoline, kerosine and hay. As they neared the church, they shouted, "Allahu-ak-bar." The Christians who were ignorant of the plot reacted sharply. A fracas ensued. Someone called a few unprepared policemen, and armed with tear gas, they dispersed the people.

But the Moslems regrouped and came back en masse. The Moslems had targeted one particular tribe, which as a unit had rejected Islam in the pre-colonial era and embraced Christianity. They hated this tribe with a perfect hatred for identifying with the enemy of Islam. The Moslems moved their attack to Tafawa Balewa, a town which was 90 percent Christian. This town is about a two-hour drive from Bauchi. Well-trained, well-armed, hefty men were driven down in lorries by the hundreds.

Before their arrival, the 10 percent Moslem population was notified and evacuated without the knowledge of the Christian tribe. Most of the jihadists also had all kinds of charms tied over their bodies. These charms were to protect them from arrows, gunshots and knife stabs. Suddenly, they descended on the town from all directions, attacking everybody in sight. The Christians were summoned in different places by church bells. The men of the town stood to defend their wards. A battle ensued and continued for three hours and fifteen minutes. There was a serious "power" play. The highly technical charmed Moslem fighters, when shot at directly, turned into snakes or bees or something scary.

As the battle continued, the police tried in vain to quiet the riots. The Christians came out en masse. While some were praying at different hideouts, others were fighting. This combination of prayer and effort from the Christians confused the Moslems, who subsequently lost their confidence and their charms failed to transform them continuously into different animals. Therefore, they ran in confusion in different directions. Unfortunately, they were all hired killers and did not know how to escape from the town, so they were all arrested by the Christian tribesmen. At the end of it, about 458 hired killers died in Tafawa Balewa. Once again, the Lord gave the Christians great victory.

The Moslem loss in Tafawa Balewa infuriated the Moslem policemen, so they took about twenty-four dead bodies of Moslems to Bauchi and laid them at the city square. When news got to the Moslem strongmen in Bauchi of their losses, the already stirred city became even more muddled. At about 7:30 p.m. on Monday, April 21, 1991, the Moslems launched a door-to-door attack on the highly unsuspecting Christians, who had not even heard of the previous day's attack at Tafawa Balewa.

The Moslems went on a systematic killing spree. All churches within the Moslem-dominated areas of the city were set ablaze. One strategic Christian strongman, a medical doctor, was rounded up in his hospital. He escaped, but the hospital was set ablaze. He ran to the house, and on his way home, he was stopped by one group. Since the whole city was mobilized and there were companies of killers all over the city, he was asked to stop his car. He did and was slapped across the face. The commander of the company rebuked the person who slapped him, saying, mockingly, "How can you slap a big man like him? He is an important man. Allow him to come down from his car so that he will eat his own flesh gradually until he dies." This man, Dr. Bukata, was at that time the Bauchi State Commissioner of Health.

As they were preparing to cut him up in pieces, he asked for permission to pull off from the road. He revved his Mercedes Benz car engine and drove over some of the killers, killing about four people. He drove his car directly into the army barracks. With his escape, the company headed straight to his house and took his mother and pounded her into a mass of flesh like you would mash potatoes. Two of his sons and his house maid were locked up in the house and set ablaze. His wife was not at home, so she escaped.

Engineer Bulus, the Director-General of Works for Bauchi state and a committed Christian, was slaughtered in front of his wife and children and his house was set on fire.

Another man and his family were rounded up in their home and set ablaze. As the mob moved from one street to the next, they left a sea of blood all over the road. Dead bodies were lying everywhere. Some of the dead bodies were headless. The Moslems had taken the heads away for charms. Dozens of people disappeared completely. Some corpses lost their tongues, eyes, sexual organs and other bodily internal organs. For about two weeks the city, though having been cleared of all dead bodies, still carried the odor of blood and the stench of dead bodies.

The total number of churches that were burned and destroyed were twenty-six: Three ECWA churches, six COCIN churches, three Deeper Life churches, three Baptist churches, one Redeemed Peoples Mission church, one Peculiar Peoples church, two Lutheran churches, three Anglican churches and four Roman Catholic churches.

A large number of homes belonging to Christians were burned in their totality in some sections of the town. Christians who were renting Moslem houses were sent packing, their belongings looted or vandalized. As if this was not enough, all the Christians who ran from their burning homes and properties to the army barracks, the Moslem jihadists followed them to the barracks to make sure they were all killed. All the killing, looting, vandalism and burning took place in one night.

By the next day, the city of over 300,000 people was completely deserted. It looked more like a ghost town. Thousands of people lost their lives to the Moslem jihadists. There was no governmental intervention to stop the murderers, simply because the governor, who was a Moslem and the chief security officer to the state, refused to give the police or the military any orders to arrest the situation, in spite of all the efforts made by leaders of the Christian Association of Nigeria in Bauchi to get him to act. All three key men of authority, who should have issued orders to stop the bloodshed, were Moslems. Nothing could be done. The Christians were left at the mercy of the killers and God's security. The killers had their fill of blood.

Very nauseating stories were told of how people were slaughtered like chickens, and the killers used the blood of their victims to wash their heads and face. Some even licked their victim's blood. By the time this news reached the nation, all were inflamed to the extreme. Government media houses, however, were not allowed to carry the story of the massacres. The government never issued any straightforward statement about the massacres. Until the present time, no one has ever been charged for this wildness.

On Wednesday, the 24th, of that same week, because the government did nothing about the two days of killings in Bauchi, Moslems in other counties of Bauchi state moved on the Christians in their villages, killing, looting burning, maiming, and vandalizing. In the town of Ningi, a Christian policeman was killed and the police station where he was a divisional police officer, was burned down. Several churches were burned down. In Bununu district, two churches were burned down.

Kano City Nightmare

October 14, 1991, was to be the first night of the greatest crusade Reinhard Bonnke had ever held in the whole of Africa. An estimated crowd of over 750,000 people was expected. As part of the preparations, handbills and posters were printed in Arabic, since the majority of the people in a city of almost four million people would identify with the Arabic writing as Moslems.

Every Moslem man is normally married to four women to prove he is a real man and in fulfillment of the Islamic convictions. These women and their children, especially girls, are not allowed to go out anywhere. The man always keeps the wives away from the normal society to avoid temptations and the possibility of promiscuity. Their compounds are usually fenced. This posed as a very difficult obstacle for the distribution of the handbills, so we decided to go by air into such locked-in compounds with the use of helicopters. The helicopters poured hundreds and thousands of these bills into the locked compounds of these captive women.

The previous year, Bonnke had a crusade in Kaduna and the program was attended by over 500,000 people. Most of those who were healed were Moslems. The Moslems who experienced the power of God firsthand, would without delay accept Christ and switch religious camps. Since this crusade, the Kano Moslems were greatly infuriated. Following the announcement that such a crusade was to be held in Kano, the Moslems held all kinds of meetings on how to stop the crusade since they believed that Kano state was a Moslem state.

They were afraid of the same experience of the Kaduna crusade repeating itself in Kano — the healings and the mass conversion of Moslems to Christianity. The first place of attack was the venue of the crusade. They first approved the use of the government ground at the cost of about $3,000 a night, then changed it to $4,000 a night, and at the last moment, the approval was cancelled. So the crusade was moved to the football field of the St. Thomas church compound. Yet, the Moslems would not allow the crusade to go on.

Being a Moslem state, all of the strategic government officers were Moslems — the emir, the police commissioner, the commander of the army cantonment, the governor. Everything was Moslem-controlled.

So, on the afternoon of October 14, 1991, Moslems caught a heavily pregnant Christian woman, took her to the front of the army headquarters and laid her on the rough ground and ripped her open from her neck down to her anus with a knife (like you would split open a slaughtered bull to bring out its internal organs), exposing all her internal organs. The unborn child was smashed. Of course, the woman and the child died instantly. The army chief said nothing. Because it was a planned thing, all the chief law enforcement officers were told not to give orders to their forces to intervene. So the Moslems all over the city went on their usual jihad, cutting off Christians' heads, opening up pregnant women, like the one described above, looting, burning churches, attacking the homes of pastors and all strategic Christian leaders.

A black cloud settled over the city as a result of the burnings, looting and bloodshed. Soon the jihad spread all over the whole state. Moslems were shouting, "Clean out the state of all kafiris (infidels)." Clean the state they did. All that belonged to anyone who was not a Moslem was either burned, damaged, or looted. Cars were burned or seized, shopping malls were vandalized. Buildings with stickers or signs of the cross were pulled down and burned. People were locked up in homes and set ablaze until they burned to ashes. The whole city was littered with headless bodies, or bodies with some major organs missing.

Christian schools were razed, and pupils were attacked. Many cases of missing children were reported, quite possibly stolen by Moslems for Islamic rituals.

Before the killings, the Moslems were said to have been meeting and conducting special training sessions for the killing, looting and vandalizing squads. Since the chief law enforcement officers were Moslems, nothing was done to arrest the training or the killing. Neither soldiers nor policemen were discharged to the troubled areas until the Moslems had finished their killings and quenched their thirst for blood before they were commanded to kill all lawless people at sight. This was about the time when the Christians had organized pockets of resistance.

At the end of the jihad, the government set up a committee to look into the happening. To this date, some five years later, nothing has been said or done by government. As I told you in an earlier chapter, Moslems hold fellow Moslems at a higher value than non-Muslims.

Over 10,000 lives were lost in the jihad, over 100 churches and Christian businesses were burned down and over 100 vehicles were destroyed.

The Beheading of Brother Gideon Akaluka

On December 25, 1994, an innocent Christian brother was arrested by the Moslem authority, taken to a Moslem-controlled government prison in Kano and beheaded by a Moslem jihadist. They falsely accused him of using pieces of the Koran as toilet paper. They used a hand saw to cut off his head. Following is the true account as told by Gideon's brother.

Gideon Akaluka is my brother of the same father and mother. He came to Kano to earn his own living around April, 1994. Barely after a month in Kano, we sent a message to him to come home because of our father's sickness. He did come at the end of May, 1994. He stayed at home for four months until our father died. Gideon came back to Kano at the end of October, 1994. Sometime in November, the first week of the month, while he was in his shop, somebody informed him that something was happening in the compound where he lived in Kano.

As he arrived at his compound, the police and his landlord asked him to enter a vehicle. He asked them why. They replied that they wanted to save his life! Personally, I got to hear about the arrest and detention of Gideon when some people traveled home. At the end of November, 1994, I quickly rushed to Kano. On my arrival, I found out that a lawyer tried to get Gideon's bail, some concerned persons also made efforts, all in vain. I could not get my brother out. Therefore, I got another lawyer who took me down to the Goron-Dutse prison where my lawyer and I were allowed to see my brother. He narrated to me how he was brought to the prison as earlier described.

I had to rush back home where I informed our relations of the condition of Gideon. I spent ten days at home and then returned to Kano. I checked all the possible courts, first Kasuwa Upper Area Court where the prosecutors and judges told my lawyer point blank that they could not bail him out because of the serious nature of the case.

I was helpless and then went to the prison again with my former lawyer who was ready to assist. We talked with Gideon and Joseph, who informed us of how they were being maltreated by the prison authorities. On my third visit, even my lawyer was refused permission to see Gideon.

My former lawyer then wrote a letter to the Military Administrator and copied it for the A. G., C. J. and Commissioner of Police dated December 13, 1994. I learned that there was a meeting on the issue. We waited to no avail, as nothing was forthcoming from the government. I then traveled home to inform our relations of what had been happening. I instructed my lawyer to meet the Eze Ndi-Ibo (the chief of Ibos in Kano) for further action before I came back, but he refused, saying his steps were purely judicial.

I came back on the December 20, 1994, and my lawyer filed papers at the Dedera High Court on December 21, 1994. The order for the release of Gideon and one other person was granted on December 22, 1994, and it was served on the police and Abdullahi Yahaya, Esq., a superintendent of police on that same date.

My lawyer and I tried in vain to get their bail that day. The next day, we were told to come back after Christmas. I seriously suspected that they had already planned to kill Gideon. That is why we were informed to come after Christmas. They had indeed achieved their aim.

I happened to find out that the property which belonged to Gideon, a motor spare part dealer, was looted from the house where he lived. The police did not care to take any security measures to protect his life and properties, including the money for his business, which was in his room. At the time of his arrest, he informed me that he had 30,000 naira, one golden chain, one wrist watch (golden) and a bangle and shoe, which were deposited with the prison authorities.

Thank you, sir.

Yours Faithfully,

Samuel Akaluka

After Gideon was beheaded, his head was hoisted on a pole and carried around Kano city by a crowd of thousands of Islamic fanatics in a festive, high-spirited ceremony. The police saw this cannibalistic celebration, but did nothing about it.

According to Suratut-Tauba, verse 12 of the Quran, the Moslem is commanded to fight and war against all non-Muslim establishments. So, during this occasion, all Christians who were renting houses from Muslims were sent out from these Moslem homes.

Their belongings were confiscated or looted. The government said nothing and did nothing! All efforts made by the Christian Association of Nigeria (CAN) to get the government to react and take some action met with resistance and disregard.

Kano Again — May 30, 1995

Trouble started along Hausa/Ibo Road by Russel Avenue where two people, Mr. Authur Nwankwo and mallam Abubakar Abdu, were engaged in a fight because of theft committed by two Moslem boys. Mr. Nwankwo, a Christian, raised an alarm. This angered the people of the Islamic faith, especially since the car the boys were stealing belonged to a Christian. The Moslems took it as an opportunity to again attack churches, Christian homes and businesses, just as they did in 1991. By the end of the encounter, over 3,000 people were said to be dead, excluding the many unidentified, charred or burned bodies received out of Sabon Gari by the police, REDA/Fire Brigade. A total of thirty-two motor vehicles, eighty-one motorcycles and bicycles and forty-nine shops were reported vandalized, burglarized, burned, or looted. Churches burned were valued at an estimated 23,000,000 naira. Over 3,000,000 naira of property was damaged. Over 200,000,000 naira consumable items belonging to Christians were damaged.

These same jihads have been carried out all over Northern Nigeria, including Kaduna, a city of over 2,500,000 people where thousands of lives were lost, churches burned and Christian homes vandalized. The same thing happened in Zaria, Potiskum and many other places too numerous to list in this book.

The symbol of the two crossed swords and the crescent of the moon should teach every reasonable human being that Islam is a religion of war, violence and death. The moon represents the killings that must take place, mostly in the night for Islam to possess a place. Islam enters initially quietly, then it starts setting peoples and families against themselves, breaking their confidence in one another, so disciples are raised for Islam. Gradually, the converts are convinced and drilled to believe that they must take the land by force.

Moslems brag that they are soon going to convert or overrun Christian America and the West. If they can't do it in peace, they will buy up sensitive businesses or they will use the crude oil resources to bring the Christian nations to their knees.

Unrestricted Man Hunting

Mallam Yusufu Mohammed Abdul was a Moslem for about forty-eight years of the first part of his life. He used to listen to open air preachers of the Christian faith once in a while and that only by the roadside while passing. From his Islamic upbringing, he was taught to hate Christians for serving three Gods and for lying about the prophet Isa (Christ) by claiming that Isa is the Son of God, whereas Isa Himself never made such claims. So, he hated Christians with a perfect hatred. He even joined the jihad squad in one of the thickly Moslem populated states in Nigeria. He belonged to the Izala sect, which is known to be the most fanatical of all the Islamic sects in Nigeria. He participated in preparing young men who killed and maimed Christians in some major cities in Northern Nigeria. He recalls how they used to lick the blood of their victims as a sign of superiority.

He remembers giving instructions for eyeballs, tongues, sexual organs and brain tissues to be removed from bodies during their jihad operations. These human spare parts were used in making all kinds of medicinal concoctions.

One time as he was confronting a pastor who was about to be beheaded during a jihad, he asked the pastor to deny Christ and say, "Mohammed is the only prophet of God, and Jesus is not the Son of God." In spite of the fact that the pastor saw the machete that would take off his head with only one swing, the pastor refused to recant. Instead, he looked at his killer and said, "I love you, and Jesus shall make you preach in my place for His Gospel."

When the pastor finished making his statement, they chopped off his head with one swoop of the machete. After he left the site of the killing, that pastor's words kept haunting him. He could not sleep well any night after that.

One day he was in the mosque during an odd time to pray and meditate together with some of his disciples. Suddenly, there was a large image of someone on the wall in front of them. The image looked like the popular pictures of Christ he was used to seeing on posters displayed in shops. The man in the image said in Arabic, "I am the Christ you are persecuting, but go to the pastor of such-and-such a church (name withheld for security reasons) and he will tell you what you must do to be saved. If you want to enter heaven, you cannot get there praying the type of prayer you are praying now."

So he went to the pastor as he was directed. Immediately, he gave his life in an intense spirit of repentance. He was baptized in the Spirit. He went through weeks of training. I took him in some special training sessions. This man became a fire brand. As soon as the news about his conversion was revealed, his extremist Izalla sect started looking for him. By then, he was well hidden, together with some of his disciples who repented with him. His home was vandalized, his wives were taken away, his children were put to death. He virtually lost everything but his life.

Another case that comes to mind is the case of a man who, after his conversion, was caught by militant Islamic family members and brutally manhandled, beaten with clubs and his head pounded with iron rods. An eye popped out while being beaten. He lost an ear and was thrown into a pit and left for dead. However, he was found by some Christians who took him to the hospital where he was treated for over fifteen months before he fully recovered consciousness and health, not without some disability.

Some of us ministers in Northern Nigeria have had to escape for our lives several times. My children have been rounded up for the kill by Moslems several times, but by some strange miracles, they were always delivered.

A lady in her sixties, a devout Moslem, was sleeping in her house when she suddenly felt a very strong presence and woke up. The husband, who was lying by her side, noticed it and woke up to find her talking to someone. She described this person as the most beautiful man she ever saw. He was radiant in complexion, his hair was long and falling over his shoulders. His eyes were as fire piercing through her whole being. Before he opened his mouth to speak to her, she already knew what he was going to say. He made her understand him instantly without confusion.

The first day, he took her to this most beautiful place. With the touch of his hand, they would just appear in this fair and beautiful country. These appearances took place three times. The second time of his appearance she asked the man his name. The man told her it was not yet time for her to know his name. He promised to tell her when the time was right. The third visit was a correctional visit. He told her about some happenings that were about to take place with her husband and children. These things came to pass as she was told. This third time he told her she was about to change her direction in life, and it was going to affect her dramatically, because she was going to have to stand against fiery tests and persecution. But he promised to be with her. He told her to go and see a certain devoted Christian lady, who would tell her his name and also tell her about how to gain admission into the place he had been showing her in his visits. She would also tell her how to pray correctly to God, the Father of all.

The devout Moslem lady left to see the Christian sister as soon as it was morning, narrating all that she had been seeing. The sister told her the man she was seeing was Jesus Christ. The place she was taken to was called heaven, and to get there she had to be born again and thoroughly converted. The Moslem lady repented and was baptized immediately.

All hell broke loose when her people discovered that she had changed her religion. She had inherited some parcels of land from her parents, but they were all confiscated. All her clothing, jewelry and houses were confiscated. However, she stuck with Christ. Her eyes had seen too much of Christ and of heaven for any persecution to turn her away from believing in Him. She is presently still working for Christ, whom she has seen with her own eyes.

I am also reminded of some supernatural interventions God wrought on behalf of believers in some cities where they were being attacked by Moslems without provocation. Most jihads they had staged were either because some strategic Moslem was converted or out of some strange thirst for blood and the hatred that desires to wipe out all other religions from their environment, except Islam. In this small town called Ibi, during the early 1990's the Islamic fanatics opened persecution against the church. This small town was not far away from Bauchi city where the heaviest Christian casualties in a Moslem jihad were incurred. Six months after the Bauchi jihad, God visited some parts of Bauchi and Ibi with some mysterious fires. Moslem homes were selected and burned down by a strange type of fire. The flames could not be seen with the eye. All you saw was heat, but no smoke. The fire fighting department tried to fight the flames. The more they applied water, the hotter the flames got. In some cases, the fire would enter into trunk boxes and burn clothes, jewelry and other metallic utensils in the house, yet the house was left intact.

In both towns, not one Christian home was burned. If a Christian's home was in between two Moslem houses, the fire jumped the Christian house and burned the next Moslem home. Houses that were not razed to the ground had all their useful materials burned. A woman would come home from work to find the house securely locked as they left it in the morning only to discover that everything in the house was burned to ashes, but the roof was left intact.

The same Moslem leaders called on church leaders with one voice to pray for their people that God would forgive them and remove the strange fire. So churches fasted and prayed and asked God to stay His anger. God answered and the fire was stopped from spreading beyond the two cities. But as it looked, God intended to really visit the whole of Northern Nigerian Moslems with this strange fire.

After the incident of the strange fire, the son of the Sultan was said to have converted to Christianity. He said God told him to visit a few Christian leaders in Northern Nigeria and receive instruction from them. I was one of those he claimed God told him to visit. This man had such a sweet tongue, he could talk you into selling yourself to him without pay. He could easily gather fellowship. He said so many swelling things about Christians rising up to fight for their rights. He made very powerful statements about Christ and against Mohammed.

When he started visiting me for the so-called training periods as God directed, I started receiving a check in my spirit about him. I would give him surprise visits in his house and find him with all kinds of girls. Surprisingly, he never had any persecution from his Moslem people. To be converted to Christianity from the first Moslem family in Nigeria and not to be persecuted was too much for me to understand. The Sultan of Sokoto is the final authority on all Islamic matters in Nigeria and some neighboring countries. For his son to be converted and not be persecuted was strange.

Gradually, he gained entrance into churches by using names of those Christian leaders he had met. He was speaking some great swelling words about liberating the church from the clutches of jihadists. He wanted to know all that makes Christianity what it is. His teachable attitude gained him a lot of acceptance. Many hearts were turned to him, and many people had a lot of hope in him.

With prayers for him going up to God from sincere hearts of believers, the chaff in him came to the surface. During a private prayer for him, the power of God hit him and he confessed that he was only sent as a spy to know Christianity experientially and also know how to destroy it from within by planting discord in the leadership of different denominations; to lure young Christian girls to marry Moslem boys in different states; and to create confusion between Christian groups. He was not persecuted because he was on a Moslem-assigned errand.

Mohammed's Mind

To understand why Islam is a spirit of violence, you need to understand the mind of its chief founder. Robert Payne in his book, *The Holy Sword*, says:

> "It is worthwhile to pause for a moment before the quite astonishing polarity of Mohammed's mind. Violence and gentleness were at war within him. Sometimes he gives the

*appearance of living within two worlds...For the rest, his
character seems, like that of many another, to have been a
strange mixture. He was a poet rather than a theologian; a
master improviser rather than a systematic thinker. He was
generous, resolute, genial and astute; a shrewd judge and a
born leader of men. He could, however, be cruel and vindictive
to his enemies, he could stoop to assassination, and he was
undeniably sensual."*

To expect a better life from Mohammed would be like
asking the leopard to change its spots. Mohammed was an
ordinary man, just as any other. He lived a life of violence
and left an example for his band of followers to do likewise.
A true prophet of God or a Savior from God teaches
His people to shun vengeance and run from self-motivated
violence. Jesus, the Son of God, taught against violence and
vengeance.

Christ Apostolic Church and vehicles destroyed
Majimiyar C.A.C. da motocin da aka kona

COCIN Church Railway, Bauchi
Majamiyar COCIN ta Railwa Bauchi

Christian residential areas and property destroyed and
looted in the name of God
Mazaunin masu bi da kayayakin su aka kona da
wasoso cikin Sunan Allah

Lives not spared!
Rayuka ma sun shiga uku!

Burnt Catholic Church
Konanen Majamiyar ta Katolika

An E.C.W.A. Church not spared
Majamiyar E.C.W.A. da aka kona

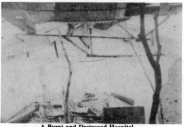

A Burnt and Destroyed Hospital
Asibiti in da ake Shan Magani ma an lalatar

Bauchi State Christian Pilgrimage Board destroyed
A lalatar da Hukumar Mahajata ta Kirista a Bauchi

Bishara Baptist Church, Bauchi

Assembly of God Church burnt and destroyed

Deeper Life Bible Church burnt
An kona Majamiyar Deeper Life

One of the COCIN Churches razed
Daya daga cikin Majamiyun COCIN da aka kona

COCIN Centre Bauchi burnt
Majamiyar COCIN da aka kona

A vehicle burnt by Islamic mob
Wata moto wanda masalata sun kona

9

Jesus in Islam

Jesus (Isa) is spoken of in the Muslim book, the Qur'an, some thirty-five times, and yet it is on this question of the works and person of Jesus that fundamental Christians and Moslems have been diametrically divided for centuries. In this chapter, I will quote extensively from Geoffrey Parriender's informative book, *Jesus in the Qur'an,* to help us understand other deceptive aspects of Islam.

Theoretically, every honest Muslim enquirer should be able to find and strike a personal relationship with Jesus Christ from the teachings of the Qur'an. However, in the course of Islamic history, various attitudes have been adopted towards Jesus. Some of these are based on the Qur'an itself, while others have been influenced by later commentaries on the controversies that have made Islam and Christianity enemies rather than allies. There have been some attempts of dialogue among the liberal camps of both faiths, to try and find a common path because it would appear their origin is one. That was the intention of Geoffrey Parriender, and as if he wanted to pacify the Muslim, he had this to say:

> Many of the early Muslim writers had studied and appreciated the Bible, Old and New Testaments. But later centuries widened the gap between the religions and their scriptures. Crusades and holy wars, inquisitions and perse-

cutions, alienated those who should have been 'nearest in love' to one another.

In Islam there is clearly a mystery about Jesus. It was accepted generally that His birth was unusual, comparable only with that of Adam.

Jesus would be the only man in history who had not died. The stark tragedy of the crucifixion reveals depths of the human and divine natures that remain unapprehended. Yet the challenge remains to search for the truth of the revelation of love and the relationship of God to men which appeared in the person of Christ. "What think ye of Christ?" is still a question to be answered. To the Christian also there is a challenge.

It is too easily assumed that all traditional doctrines are firmly based on the Bible. The Semitic view of God may need to be cleared of some Greek theories that have overlaid it. Then, if theology is to make contact with the modern world, it must express itself in a meaningful way. Terms like *Son of God, Trinity* and *salvation* need to be re-shaped and given new point. Concepts of prophecy, inspiration and revelation must be re-examined in view of the undoubted revelation of God in Mohammed and in the Qur'an. Then much more real charity and generous understanding must be shown to members of other faiths. The example of Islam towards other "people of the Book" often puts us to shame. Christians always need to remember the words of Jesus, *"And why call ye me, Lord, Lord, and do not the things which I say?"* (Luke 6:46 KJV). It is to encourage study, self-examination, dialogue and searching the Scriptures that this book has been written.

If Muslims had shown half of the tolerance and understanding Jews and Christians (people of the Book) have shown to them over the years, there would have been so much peace in the world that there would be no need for the United Nations. Many Christians have forgotten that Syria and North Africa were once the heartland of the Christian world (people of the Book)! But during the first Islamic invasion in the years 632 to 732 A.D., they were over-run and fell under Arab control. Muslim armies swept into Western Europe and stood no more than 200 kilometers south of Paris and near Geneva. If Charles Martel had not stood firm, we would all likely be Muslims today! Buetzsche, the atheist, ventured to say sarcastically, "The greatest mistake in world history was the defeat of the Arabs at Tours and Poitiers."

A vast ignorance prevails in this sphere of tolerance. Philanthropists try to solve the problem superficially with well-meaning programs, dialogues, suggestions and liberal theology, but they are not getting to the root of the problem. Islam is an evil spirit which thrives on the use of force, com-pulsion, obligation and the law. The converts will initially be enticed physically through material gifts and promises of more. The gullible materialist will then find himself exposed to the activities of seducing demons. The multitudes of regulations in Islam are only a coverup to the polluting effects of these demons.

Jesus is spoken of some thirty-five times in the Qur'an. The post hijra to medina Suras as from A.D. 622 are 2, 3, 4, 5, 9, 33, 57 and 61. The Qur'an sees Jesus in the mirror of a theological milieu which believes that every community has a messenger from God. That immediately gives recognition to other compatible religions as part of the general revela-tion of God but distinct from the special or prophetic revelation of theirs. However, "abrogation" as a method of interpretation for the Qur'an is the most deadly weapon hindering Muslims from seeing Jesus in the Qur'an as Lord and Savior. The tool makes every scripture relative.The hermeneutical tool of "abrogation" operates best when two verses in the Qur'an are in contradiction. The verse which appeals to the interpreter "abrogates" the "offensive" verse.

Therefore, a verse may have a lofty and sound theological pronouncement on Jesus in the Qur'an, but another,
probably from the post-Meccan Suras, will say the vilest
thing about Jesus. This later verse abrogates the first verse
and its interpretation takes precedence. There is no system
or scheme to help interpreters know beforehand which verse
abrogates the other. The tool is very subjective. It has been
used as wool covering to blind the eyes of many Muslims
who would otherwise have seen Jesus in the Qur'an.

One of the most common titles for Jesus in the Qur'an
is Son of Mary (Ibn Maryam) without question. Its chief
objection is to the term, *Son of God*. Jesus receives the title
Messiah (Christ) eleven times in the Qur'an, all the Median
Sura. It appears to have a particular meaning, only a messenger of God and is different from the Christian usage.

Jesus is called *servant of God* in the Qur'an, highlight-
ing His submission and worship of God. The relationship is
religious rather than social. Jesus is also called a prophet in
company with other prophets and figures of old. A prophet
is a messenger of a particular kind, chosen for a special purpose with a message from God. The prophets brought the
books of divine revelation. The title messenger or apostle
(rasul) is used ten times of Jesus in the Qur'an. They bring
good tidings and warning, so that the people should have
no argument against God. Jesus was sent as a messenger, in
succession to the earlier messengers. Jesus is spoken of as
Word in certain passages. He came into existence by God's
command without a father, a new creation.

Jesus is also called the *Spirit* seven times in the Qur'an.
The birth of Jesus in the Qur'an was brought about by the
plain but powerful word of God. He said "Be!" and it was.
The Quran does agree that Jesus was born as "Isa Ruhun
Lahi" — that is, Jesus was born of the Holy Ghost.

However, this by no means, as far as Muslims are concerned, makes Jesus superior. The creation of Adam is cited
as a support. However, the early Muslims' rejection against
physical begetting of Christ is within the context of their

opposition to the pagan attribution of wives and children to their gods, Al-lat, Al-uzza and Manat.

Teachings of Jesus are in the Gospel, and the Qur'an does not repeat them. What does the Qur'an mean in its words about the death of Jesus? Muslims deny that Jesus died. They believe He will die only after His second coming (Sura 4:156-157), that Jesus would return and live for forty years. Then He will die and be buried by Muslims at Medina.

That is reading far too much into the Qur'an. Some of the passages as 4:154-157/155-159 were meant to defend the Messiah against the Jews, who maintained that they alone had killed and crucified Him, and therefore that He could not be the Messiah. Did Jesus really die on the cross? Was there a substitute who suffered in His place? There is no doubt that the canonical gospels all affirm the first and have no suggestion of the second. Muslims got their story of substitute death from a gospel written by the Egyptian gnostic Christian, Basilides, who lived in the second century.

They alleged Simon of Cyrene was the substitute. Some suggested the widow of Nain's son. Judas, Pilate, a disciple, or even an enemy of Jesus had also been suggested. That Jesus cast His likeness on Judas to be crucified, but the real Judas committed suicide and Jesus went up to heaven. All these are mere romancing, and there is nothing scriptural about them. The idea of a substitute has been taught for ages by Muslims.

We should also bear in mind that Islam is a post-Christian religion. Out of historical necessity, Mohammed had to come to terms with the Christ of the New Testament. He accepted Christ partially, yet denied some crucial factors of His life to create space for his own religion. The christology of Islam is a false standard which they use to measure our Savior and His salvation. We must recognize the fact that 600 years after the supernatural birth of His only Son, God would not have sent the angel Gabriel to Mecca to tell Mohammed that He, the living God, has no Son! The purpose of Christ's birth is to die on the cross to take away the sins of the world, and God cannot turn around and deny it. If Islam claims that Mohammed received real inspiration, then it was another spirit, a false spirit, and not the Holy Spirit Who inspired Mohammed. God does not lie. (See Numbers 23:19.)

Finally, let's say a word on the claims that Mohammed can be found in the gospels according to Parriender.

It has often been suggested that Parakletos, *Comforter*, was confused with Periklutos, *celebrated*. Since *celebrated* or *praised* is the meaning of Ahmad, commentators and editors have assumed that Ahmad was predicted in the Gospel by name. But it is hard to substantiate this. There is no mention of Ahmad in Sura 61:6. Secondly, neither Ibn Isahq nor Ibn Hishim, who edited and enlarged the life of Mohammed later, made any reference to Sura 61. Both writers, of course, knew the Qur'an well, and they often quoted it in appropriate contexts. The implication is that neither Ibn Hishim nor his predecessor knew anything about the surmised reading as Ahmad.

Their concern was not for any similarity in name. Guillaume, in his translation of Ibn Ishaq, notes that his quotation of the gospel (John 15:23ff) is taken from the Palestinian Syriac Lectionary and not from the ordinary Bible of the Syraic-speaking churches. The lectionary renders *Comforter* whereas all other Syraic versions render *Paraclete* following the Greek. The Munahhemana means "lifegiver," but in this context it must mean a "consoler" or "comforter." Ibn Ishaq's virtual identification of this name with Mohammed is undoubtedly stretching resemblance rather far. More to the point is his reference to the coming of the Spirit of truth.

Every honest seeker of the truth must look for Jesus Christ in the Gospel, New Testament, and not elsewhere.

10
How To Help a Moslem Find and Understand Christ

Every Muslim professes to believe in Jesus, but it is "another Jesus." The "Isa" of the Koran is only one prophet among 124,000. He was sent only to the Jews. He was not the Son of God. He denied the Trinity. He was born of the Virgin Mary, but Gabriel was his father, according to Bedami (a Koranic interpreter in A.D. 1282, who wrote many books on Islamic theology). While still a small baby, He spoke; and when He was a child, He made a clay bird and caused it to live and fly.

He was created of the dust as was Adam. He healed the blind and cleansed the lepers and had power to raise the dead, but this was only by God's permission. He foretold the coming of Mohammed. He cursed Israel. He was not crucified and did not die; it only seemed so to man. He lives today and will return to this earth where He will marry, have children, and die at Medina where He will be buried in a prepared grave beside that of Mohammed. He will reign for forty years and will establish Islam in the whole world.

Is this Isa our glorious Lord, or another Jesus? Some would suggest that by substituting the name "Yesu" for "Isa," we can present a compromise acceptable to all.

Experience has shown that this change of name affects little. We must put the correct content into the Word. This can only be done by our teaching, preaching and conversation. Whichever name is used, the Christian worker should never speak of Anebi "Isa" or "Isa Al Masihu," but always give Jesus His title of Lord. This will be Rabbana or Sayyidna. He is Sayyidna Al Masihu (our Lord Christ).

We must now face the fact that the Koran categorically denies the two outstanding truths of the Gospel:

1. The deity of Christ.

2. His atoning death.

Communicating the Truth
Concerning the Son of God

Let us consider how one can avoid communicating a lie though insisting on the truth. When the Moslem asks, "Was Jesus the Son of God?" we must never give an un-qualified, affirmative reply. Rather, respond, "Who do you understand the term *Ibn Allah* to be? i.e., the Son of God?"

He will probably reply, "It can have only one meaning, and that is that God went to bed with a woman and a baby was born." He has stated the lie in his mind. No Christian in all the world believes that. It is absolute blasphemy. We Christians dare not express such a thought. We must then be prepared to communicate the truth.

Let us remember that Moslems accuse us of making a man God. We must remind them that we never attempt to do this. The Bible teaches that God became man. The eternal Word became flesh. The movement is from above and goes downward, not from below moving upward. (See John 1:1-18; Philippians 2.)

We must tell them what the Bible says about Christ and not try to dilute it or manage it. It is only when a man agrees and believes that Jesus is the Son of God, and that He died on the cross to save us as individuals, that he can find salvation. The absence of this belief brings instant condemnation. So, let's not try to create compromises to make it easier for the Moslem. He must denounce all the incorrect views of the Koran about Christ and believe the truth of the Bible.

"He who believes in Him [who clings to, trusts in, relies on Him] is not judged [he who trusts in Him never comes up for judgment; for him there is no rejection, no condemnation — he incurs no damnation]; but he who does not believe (cleave to, rely on, trust in Him) is judged already [he has already been convicted and has already received his sentence] because he has not believed in and trusted in the name of the only begotten Son of God. [He is condemned for refusing to let his trust rest in Christ's name]" (John 3:18).

Many people seem to believe that, first of all, the Bible has to be explained, but that is not true. It has to be believed and obeyed! We fail to see the tremendous difference between knowing the Word of God and knowing the God of the Word. No matter the explanations you try to offer to a man who has made up his mind to be sceptical, he will remain unchanged. If he ever is changed it will be by God's miraculous ways.

Allah's Omnipresence and the Qiblah

The erroneous understanding of Muslims about the true Almighty God was strongly founded on the transferred, shallow perception of Mohammed about God and his (Mohammed's) personal animosity against Christ.

Mohammed fully understood that the Father whom Jesus proclaimed is omnipresent and omnidirectional, but one day he just instructed his followers to stop facing other places like Jerusalem to pray, but to pray in the direction of his mosque at Mecca. From whatever point in the world, they were to face the east to say their prayers. When reactions started coming to this change, he explained that the change of "Qiblah" (direction of prayer facing Mecca) did not mean anything else but to know how many of the followers were actually loyal to him. But the real truth of the matter was that just before the change, Mohammed had transferred into the Ka'bah in Mecca the pre-Islamic Arab's "Allah" idol. Since the object of worship is the "Allah" idol, he had to instruct the change of direction of prayer. The idol is what is contained in the black square box building at the

center of the pilgrimage ground in Mecca. Innocent people
with simple minds never stop to ask why people have to go
around that spot of the pilgrimage ground. They all must be
undressed, tying only wrappers over their bodies. This is
the picture we see in the Baal worshippers of the Old Testament Bible. In fact, the Jews who were friendly with
Mohammed then, disassociated themselves from him, because they accused him of demon worship. If he really
believed God was everywhere, then all Moslems could pray
facing any direction. Christians pray facing any direction
because they believe that God is everywhere. We do not have
to face a particular direction to get His attention.

Helping the Moslem Find Christ

Assist him to find God by clearing his erroneous knowledge of the God of the Bible. If he finds the God of the Bible,
he will find Christ.

Do not work with the assumption that the Christian
and the Moslem serve the same God. You are not serving
the same God. Not only are their names different, their
nature and attributes are miles apart. Don't ever forget it.

Refrain from engaging in fruitless arguments about the
Trinity with a Moslem. His first and basic problem is to find
the God of the Bible. If he finds Him, everything else will
fall in place in its proper time.

The doctrine of the Trinity is one of the most widely
opposed Christian doctrines by the Moslems.

Spirited attempts are made by the Christian to prove
the Trinity. This will continue to be a futile activity because
the fact that they cannot grasp the truth of the Trinity points
to a fundamental misunderstanding of the doctrine of God.
When we attempt to help them understand the Trinity, we
are working under the assumption that their doctrine of God
as contained in the Koran is the same with that of the Bible.
This is totally false and misleading. Therefore, the beginning point to help the Moslem understand the Trinity starts
with his understanding of the doctrine of God as far as the

Bible is concerned. If he cannot accept the doctrine of God as outlined in the Bible, we would be wasting time and effort trying to help him understand the Trinity. For instance, consider the doctrine of Allah as outlined in the Koran.

The Moslem believes in Allah, who is unique, all-powerful and merciful to all Moslems.

His Oneness

The Moslems' dominant thought about Allah is expressed in the phrase "La illa a illa lah" (there is no God but Allah). They believe he is absolutely unique and inconceivable by man. Whatever your mind may think of, Allah is not that. This idea utterly excludes the thought of the holy Trinity. The greatest sin that man can commit is to worship anything other than Allah or to associate any other being on the same level with him. You can now begin to see what you are up against when you discuss the Trinity. The minds of most Moslems are closed. They are not listening. As far as a Moslem is concerned, you are in sin for daring to associate Allah with any other being.

The Allah of the Koran has over a hundred names. If he is not *to be known operationally* as a multi-faceted person, why know him by different names? And those names really mean different things. The Trinity doctrine of the Bible is simply the presentation of the multi-facetedness of God as Father, Son and Holy Ghost.

His Greatness

Allah akbar (Allah is Great, or more literally, God is greater) is consistently repeated in Moslem prayers. Allah is far greater than any thought that man can have of him. Because of his might and power, the Moslem must bow in worship, taking the attitude of a slave permanently. It is inconceivable for a Moslem to think of becoming a son of this Allah. He (Allah) is so great that he can do what he likes, even break his own laws. This suggests to me a high level of lawlessness in his relationship with man whom he is supposed to have created. He is unpredictable and makes it extremely difficult for his subjects to trust him.

The word *Al Qader* not only expresses his might, but whatever he decides will take place. It is useless to try and change this. He can wake up one day and decree that you should be poor, you should be a homosexual, or you should be a criminal. You cannot struggle against what he has decreed. Allah can freely override the power of choice that he has given to humans. He can effectively eliminate the "will" of man. And so man can freely transfer the onus of responsibility to Allah. When you become poor, Allah is responsible. If you cross the road carelessly and get knocked down by a car and you die, it is the doing of Allah and not the doing of your carelessness. When you were taken and subjected to slavery, Allah is responsible. Man therefore becomes irresponsible. He cannot be positioned to accept responsibility for his life and actions. This Allah breeds a lot of irresponsible slaves called humans. He is therefore attractive to people who will not accept responsibility for the gift of life.

His Mercy

Allah is gracious and merciful. He will have pity on all Moslems, even though they sin. This is an open license to a lifestyle of sin. Allah does not love all men. It is very hard for the Moslem to think of Allah as our father. He suspects that this would mean a physical fatherhood. He finds it very difficult to understand the love of God as expressed in Jesus Christ.

We need to remember that man cannot know God as Father except by a direct revelation (Matthew 11:25-27). You are therefore reminded to depend wholly on the Spirit of God as you communicate God to the Moslem.

In addition to the above briefs on the god of the Koran, it will be useful to bear in mind the following brief comparison on the theology of God in the Bible with the Koran.

In the Koran, Allah sends his prophets and messengers. He sends books, etc. He is so aloof and impersonal. He does not seem to want any direct contact with man. The reason may be that he created humans to be slaves.

In the Bible God comes Himself. Jesus Christ became man, and the Word was made flesh (John 1:14). God was in Christ reconciling the world to Himself (2 Corinthians 5:19).

In the Koran, man is committed to seek after Allah who can never really be found. He must take the initiative to seek without any assurance from God that he would be found. In the Bible God seeks man and finds him (Luke 19:10; 1 Timothy 1:15). Consider also the parables of the lost sheep and the lost coin (Luke 15:1-32). He also encourages man to search for Him, and assures that if man will seek for Him with his whole heart, he will find Him.

Islam is one of the world's religions, and in every religion, that which is stressed is what man must do for God. Man must work for salvation. He must pray, go to the holy place or mosque. He must fight to defend his helpless and hapless Allah.

In the Bible, the Gospel tells of what God has done for man *in Christ*. It contains all the overtures that God has made and is still making to bring man back to Him. It contains His promises to defend and keep those who trust Him.

In the Koran, man tries to earn life by observing a series of prohibitions and taboos: "Do this." "Don't do that."

The Bible points out clearly in the New Testament that God seeks to give man life freely. Man dies to live. Having received new life through the death and resurrection of Christ, he loves God and wants to please Him.

Understanding

A sympathetic comprehension of understanding Christian-Islamic distinctiveness is indispensable to giving an effective witness to the Moslem. We must love the Moslems but hate their violence. We must approach them with kindness and gentleness. An antagonistic approach to Islam will only confirm the Moslem more deeply in his beliefs and strengthen his prejudice against Christ and the cross. Do not start with the objectionable doctrines in your first encounter with a Muslim you want to win to Christ. Beginning from the prophets will be familiar ground; then you could move on to other more solid facts. Hopefully, a strong rapport and friendship would be established before the more difficult issues are discussed, like the Trinity and the cross.

Affection and Love

No conversion results from a spirited argument. An enemy cannot be won to salvation by force. So never see or treat the Muslim as an enemy. Handle him with great affection. This is the principal positive difference between Islam and Christianity. Moslems do not know affection at home, at work, or at school. The men live with their wives on a fleshly love and affection level, rather than agape.

The fallacies of Islam can only be defeated by definite prayer, and the holy war fought only with the sword of the Spirit, which is the Word of God. While Moslems have been wagging jihads against the church in Nigeria, the church is raising a "campaign of love, affection and service." What a contrast! Believers who live close to Moslems must be fired up in their Christian attitudes. Jesus said, *"But God commendeth his love toward us, in that, while we were yet sinners, Christ died for us"* (Romans 5:8 KJV).

We must desire the highest good of the Moslems. Christ's command was for us to love our enemies and pray for those who persecute us so we will be sons of our Father, for He sends His rain on both the just and the unjust. The day of recompense is coming.

The story is told of a man who won many converts by a definite show of love. This man, a farmer, had a Muslim neighbor who hated him. Their roads couldn't cross one another. One day the farmer, a believer, asked himself what he could do to win the friendship of this Moslem. He made up his mind one day after harvesting his yam tubers to send a large quantity to his Moslem neighbor. So he sent his wife with the yams on her head. The Moslem man caught her and gave her a severe beating. She barely escaped, and came home sobbing. The believer consoled his wife and treated her wounds, but refused to go to court over the abuse.

The next season of yam harvest, the farmer sent his wife again to give the Moslem neighbor yams. The Muslim beat her up again and cracked her head. The next season the believer foolishly repeated the act of goodness and love, and the Muslim beat the wife up again. But this time the Muslim's conscience would not let him go to bed that night. His conscience bothered him until he started screaming at midnight. People ran out from all over the neighborhood to see what was happening since the Muslim was shouting, "Come and see this man who wants to kill me." When people asked who was trying to kill him, he called the believer's name. The people asked how the farmer had tried to kill him. He said, "He is trying to kill me, not with a gun or arrow; he is trying to kill me with love and affection." Then he told how the believer had sent him yams free of charge, and he unkindly beat the believer's wife over and over. At the end of the night, the Muslim man gave his life to Christ and was baptized, along with his entire household, and joined the believer's fellowship.

The gun may win a battle or a war, but it never wins a heart. The sword may win jihads, but it never conquers and destroys the love of God in our hearts and the Kingdom of God. There is yet to be a heart that will not be won by love. There is yet to be a people who will be adamant and remain unaffected by the smallest show of affection. Show me an unconquerable kingdom, and I will show you victory with the smallest show of love.

The Moslem kingdom can be won step by step without a word, but with the show of love and compassion.

Longsuffering

Like a farmer waits patiently for his crop to mature and reach harvest, so must the Christian evangelist plant seeds of the Word and love and await a harvest among the Muslims. He may sow, while another will reap. We must, however, work in an organized manner to win the Muslims as soon as possible. We must not catch the seed sowing syndrome. Some people believe they are seed sowers only, and they lose the zeal necessary in their Christian witness to accomplish a conversion.

The period between the sowing and the reaping may be frustratingly painful. However, sowing is not a glamorous thing to do. It involves hard tilling of the fallow ground, carefully planting seeds, and remaining on the scene, adding water and fertilizer when needed. How beautiful it is to come along months later and harvest beautiful, luscious fruit on the vine. But there would be no reaping without sowing. Had the sower become discouraged in his task and called it quits, there would be no need for an army of eager reapers. We must sow in season and out of season, in tears and in joy.

Faith

Those who have done any small work among Moslems will quickly discover that discouragement is the strongest weapon the devil uses against the witness. This calls for a faith that can see beyond the sowing to the bright lights of harvest time. It is God's will for the ambassador of Christ to maintain a living, vibrant faith in the God of the impossible! If we hang up our sickles on the willow trees by the rivers of Babylon, then we are finished.

Prayer and Fasting

Prayer and fasting is the catalyst that binds the previous strategies into a functional thrust.

Prayer and fasting cause our words of witness to thrust through the heart of the unbelieving, sceptic infidel and the stubborn to produce results. I am not talking of a water or juice fast. Neither am I talking about holding a fasting retreat for Moslems. But I am talking about a lifestyle of prayer and fasting, not just a prayer conference.

Public Confession

The Moslem must be taught that Christ, not the family, the mosque, or religion, requires our loyalty. They must make public confession of Christ. In the Bible, all those who believed in Jesus in secret manifested themselves at His death. They took their sides with Him. They declared their love for Him openly. A Moslem is not really converted until he makes a public confession of Christ. The Moslem could deceive himself into wanting to remain a secret convert, instead of making his conversion public so he does not lose his life. Or he may plan to use his "secret conversion" simply to get aid. Jesus said in Matthew 10:32 that whoever is ashamed to declare His name before men, He also will be ashamed to declare his name before His Father.

What contribution do we make into the salvation of mankind by encouraging a clandestine faith for another? Perhaps we desire to make it easier for the Moslem to become a Christian. Christ promises no easier road. He took no easy road. While Christ upholds the importance and sanctity and unity of the home in the society, yet He made it clear that man's highest loyalty is to Him. A man's enemies may be the very members of his own household. A man may be called to leave his father, mother, sister, or relatives to follow Him.

Any Moslem convert knows that before you are accepted as a true Moslem, you must publicly declare, "Allah is one, and Mohammed is the prophet of Allah." Why should the Moslem convert to Christianity expect any less public declaration for Christ? They know that they could keep a double standard between Christianity and Islam, if the Christian witness is not aware that the only thing the Moslem knows will break him away from Islam is a public declaration of Christ. The Moslem secret disciple will deceive him to believe he is a secret Christian.

Where in the Bible do we find one place that teaches or encourages secret belief? Can the Church be built with secret disciples? What would have happened if all the apostles refused to stand with Christ in public for fear of their families and religious leaders? Where would Christianity be today? The only reason the Gospel is where it is today is because someone took the risk of a public declaration of Christ in spite of all the possibilities of persecution and death. In fact, they had a more difficult task to make a public profession of Christ, compared to the Moslems because of the Jewish leaders' perfect hatred for Christ and what He represented.

The fear of death or persecution is what keeps potential Moslem converts underground. The witness reaching the Moslem must be ready to help him find a place to be protected, fed and housed, providing him with a new lifestyle. We are in the process of developing strategic camps for Moslem converts, where they will live openly and confess Christ openly. If they are left to go back home, they could be drawn back to Islam or turned to secret Christians who will not be in any kind of Christian fellowship. Such secret believers cannot build the Church.

In my experience, we have found that baptizing the convert helps to establish him in his faith. It builds in him the psychological breakaway from Islam and puts him in the spot where he has to make up his mind to face the challenges ahead. Islam views baptism as a denunciation of religion, society and family, which is what they do to all their infidel converts to Islam. He is baptized in their own style and expected to cut from all family, co-workers and religion.

The convert must also be attached to a church family as soon as possible. The church should quickly integrate them into the mainstream of its activities. They should never be left alone. New friends should be attached to them. It may even be necessary to change their job and other social ties.

He should not be ostracized but be given the right hand of fellowship.

Help the black American Moslem realize that Islam did not originate from blacks but from Arabs who still regard and treat blacks as second-class people in the Arab world. Arabs believe blacks are good for nothing but to be slaves forever. Blacks were used to fight most of their jihads. They used blacks as guinea pigs for scientific research. It was a mass manslaughter of the black race. Their treatment of blacks was worse than the torture and mass killings of Hitler's gas chambers, or worse than the communist atrocities.

Christianity, on the other hand, involved the blacks before the white men ever got into it. Christ took refuge in Africa. Simon of Cyrene, a black man, helped Him carry His cross. Christ was not white. He came from the area that touches both Africa and Europe. Christianity, however, must not be valued by its geographical origin or racial affiliation, but by its claims of total salvation; its claims of transformation of life; its claims of righteousness and perfection; its claims that you can be sure of your salvation today and not have to wait until one uncertain morning after you die when you will wake up on the other side of eternity to weigh your good and bad deeds. Man has no ability to do right on his own. Our self-made righteousness is as filthy rags. And by the deeds of the law or good works shall no one be saved, lest they glory before God. The only way to be saved is to have a perfect Savior. Jesus said He is the Messiah, the Savior, the Christ, the Deliverer. He came to set the captives free, to open the prison gates and let the prisoners go free and to declare the acceptable year of the Lord's favor. Neither Mohammed, who came 600 years later, nor any present-day fallacious so-called prophets have ever claimed to be the Messiah, the Savior, or the Son of God. If Christ died and was resurrected, then we must be mad to disregard His claims of messiahship and His declaration of our need for a Savior. He said, *"For the Son of man is come to seek and to save that which was lost"* (Luke 19:10 KJV).

Everywhere there is a problem of terrorism, hijacking, or bombing, whether it is in Israel, the United States of America, Africa, Timbuktu, or Nigeria, usually the Moslems are connected to it. In the United States, they are instigating ignorant African-Americans in a racial conflict with the whites. To the unsuspecting Americans, it is a racial struggle, but to the deceptive Arab Moslem, it is set to achieve an Islamic religious jihad. Wake up, America! Cry for your nation and for your babies, for war, the real mother of all wars, is come into your midst bearing a double layer pregnancy of evil and deceit. The turbulence we are seeing in Northern Nigeria may be nothing compared to the killings that will take place if the Islamic infiltration into the United States is not checked. Moslems are sponsors, instigators, promoters and fuelers of most of the bombings, hijackings, wars and feuds that are taking place.

I can give you statistics of different nations that have been completely disorganized as soon as Islam entered and gained prominence. A serious economic downturn follows, and lives are lost by the millions. Moslems are killing millions in Algeria, Yemen, Lebanon, Palestine, Egypt, Croatia and Serbia. They are intolerant and unruly.

11
Becoming Responsible

The word responsibility is a word most people dread to hear. Such people do not understand why they cannot eat their cake and still have it. Each time they smell the presence of the big word, they run far away. They do not want to answer for anything or to anyone. They prefer to depend on somebody else, but not to be depended upon.

This can happen for two major reasons:

1. The capacity to "will" has been pummelled and rendered ineffective or inoperative.

2. There is no awareness of the value God places on life.

When man was created, he was created with a capacity to freely choose and to make his choice operative through the exercise of his "will." The will in man, therefore, represents the seat of "change." The "change" may be for good or evil. Whatever choices a human makes, if it is not actively supported by the "will," such choices are never effective or operative. When man gave in to sin, sin took over the management of the seat of "change." It sought to constantly make evil choices operative, while the good ones were rendered inoperative. Man became a slave to sin through the loss of his capacity to "will" to do good. He found himself at the center of the fight between good and evil. He knows which side he should support, but he lacks the wherewithal to effect his choice. He is like a referee who is expected to judge between two or more contestants, but lacks the authority to push through the sanctions he may award on either side. This is a hopeless and painful situation for any man to find himself in. He has no means of maintaining orderliness in his life. He becomes a drifter. He drifts with the evil winds that are blowing all around him and has no control as to the destination to which he is being taken.

The apostle Paul pictured himself in this situation at one point in his life (Romans 7:14-20). This is the picture of man under the grip of sin. For as long as sin has oversight over a man, he lacks the means to make operative changes in his life. He lacks what it takes to be responsible. His will be a continuous story of irresponsible behaviors. He is continuously pummelled by sin so that he will eventually give up fighting and accept his lot in life as a slave. You are not a slave until you agree with sin that you are. All of us, at one time or another, have found ourselves in the concentration camp of sin.

The major objective of sin is to turn us into the most willing slaves who can be produced, the most willing slaves who may ever live on planet earth. Many actively resisted the trainings of sin. They sought for a way of escape. Paul was one (Romans 7:24), and I am one. And eventually we found the *way* out of the concentration camp of sin (Romans 7:25). Jesus is the only way. It was not drugs, women, or rebellion against constituted authorities, homosexuality, or Islam. Your greatest enemy is not the white man, nor is it the black man. But your greatest enemy is sin. You need to urgently break free from sin. You can never hope to be responsible in life without breaking free from sin. You cannot fight your way out of the camp of sin on your own. Jesus has done all the fighting that needs to be done. He has paid for your freedom. Your place is to leave the camp of sin on the terms that Jesus set. He bought you at a high price.

You ask, "Why should I leave the camp of sin only to be taken to another camp?" That is a good question. The reason is simple. When you were created, you were created to be responsible to someone. You were expected to account to somebody. That "somebody" is God. You were not created to live the life that you want. Your life is not your own, and you cannot use it the way you want. God has a say as to how you live that life, and He has no apologies to offer you in that regard. Whereas sin sought to steal, kill and destroy you completely, God, through His training and restraints, will ensure you live life to the fullest (John 10:10). God will, through the gentle restraints He places on you, turn you into a responsible member of the human race.

Before you were born, God had fashioned out a purpose and a destiny for your life. In fact, when He was creating you, He ensured that you were "wired" correctly for that purpose. In other words, you are perfect for your purpose (Jeremiah 1:5-10). God made no mistake in creating you. You were organized so peculiarly to fit God's designed purpose for your life (Psalm 139:14). The only one who can destroy God's purpose for your life is *you* through your active connivance with sin. You connive with sin when you refuse to do your first duty as a soldier in captivity. That first duty is to escape from the camp of sin to the camp of God where you rightly belong. So stop looking too far away for your enemy. He is ever near you, and his name is sin. Stop imagining that there is no way of escape. There is a way. That way is Jesus Christ (John 14:6).

In Genesis 2:7, we are informed that God created man out of dust. When God was through with fashioning man, he lacked one vital resource for usefulness. That resource is life. It was only after God gave man life that he could be called upon to take on the challenge of fulfilling a purpose (Genesis 2:8). The breath of God turned man into a living soul. The life God gave to man is the critical factor that makes him different from the very soil upon which he walks. Once life is taken from him, he becomes nothing but dust. That means that right now we are nothing but glorified dust. What makes us important to God is the life God gave us. God took the risk of placing that valuable substance in the vessel of dust (2 Corinthians 4:7) because of the purpose He has defined for man to fulfill. He gave life to man to be invested in the fulfillment of the purpose of God. That means no man came to the earth without being adequately equipped for useful living. He was given a resource to invest. That resource is life. It was not given to him to be wasted in riotous living, but it was given to him to be invested in the realization and fulfillment of the purpose of God. Therefore, your greatest resource is *life*.

What you become in life is what you make of life. You have no reason to be angry with God. It is wicked for you to imagine that God sent you to earth to live a mediocre life. It is wicked for you to imagine that God is partial for giving you a white or black skin. It is wicked for you to question God as to why He made you a man or woman. It is the greatest demonstration of ungratefulness for you to ask God what He has created. It is wickedness for you to trifle with life — the greatest resource God could give to any man. Life was not given to you to be spent; it was given to you to be invested. You spend it when you are not conscious of anyone to whom you must give account. But you invest it when you know that someone will call on you to account for what was given to you. Friend, you will stand before God to tell Him what you did with the life He has given to you.

For you to get the best out of the resource He has given you, you must accept responsibility for that life (Matthew 16:25). Accepting responsibility for your life means that you recognize that you are liable to answer for what you did with the resource. That means that you will be called upon to account for your life. That means that you will not live on earth always looking for somebody else to blame for what is not working right in your life.

Responsible Parenthood

Great irresponsibility in the area of marriage and childbearing is evident the world over. All kinds of doctrines of devils are on the loose. Young people are rapidly choosing single parenthood as opposed to marriage. If a young person wants to have children, she just goes out and mates with a male of her choice. This is the lifestyle of dogs. They just keep littering babies without male parents to give these children what they need from the male influence. These children grow up to be very irresponsible, highly aggressive, possessed of the spirit of bitterness and vengeance against the society for all their parental deficiencies. That is one of the big reasons we have all kinds of killings by gunmen on the loose.

Single parenting is the devil's alternative for God's good plan of marriage and a proper home. God meant for a home to have both a daddy and a mommy. Single parenthood is definitely not God's plan, although He loves the single parents.

God planned that men should get married and raise children with their wives. Any other plan is of the devil and sinful. Proper parenting can be very demanding and taxing. Before the children get to be adults, both parents must keep sowing good efforts. Sometimes this is done as a struggle against poor finances, poor living accommodations, etc. All of these struggles can lead to a psychological, emotional and energy crisis in both the man and the woman. Personality conflicts between the couple do not make things easier. The coward father or mother will run away from home to escape such conflicts and responsibilities.

No matter how long a man runs away from these responsibilities, he will always be accountable to God. Even cowards have new responsibilities to live up to. While one is alive, he cannot keep from being responsible. The earlier you realize this, the better. The sooner you make up your mind to carry your matrimonial responsibilities, the better. Many family deserters have died miserable deaths. They ran away from home, so they had nothing to live for or even die for. Loneliness, temptations and heartbreak kill such people earlier than their time of death.

If a man is not yet ready to be responsible, he should not start getting involved with women, let alone father children. Men carry great guilt when they rush into marriage, only to discover that they were not ready.

Once our minds are made up to become parents or we enter into it before realizing what is ahead, we can't get out of it. We must work towards enjoying being parents rather than live on the sad side of life. No matter how bad a parent has been, he/she can always improve.

Parents must be caring. It takes time to be a parent. Do not be in a hurry to gather all the necessary experience. If you try and fail, try again. In our society of instant things and fast food, we must not expect to gather an instant experience in parenting. It will take time, and the maker of this burden will surely provide all the answers to the puzzle of proper parenting.

All through the Bible, men struggled to keep their families in line. Eli did and he was a priest. David was a man after the heart of God, but he also struggled through his responsibility as a father, as was evident in his overthrow by his son Absalom.

Learning to live with your family to produce responsible, well-ordered, disciplined children begins with a realistic view of your responsibilities, expectations and problems. Family life can and does work, but only in the hands of those who understand that it is a continually changing and less than perfect experience. Normal parents are not too serious to be moved to laughter or tears by their children. The family may not have a lot of money, but they can do a lot of things together. Parents can make time to attend their children's school games, and also listen to them speak their minds. Normal parents also make mistakes, but they do not run away from such mistakes. They correct them. Mistakes do not mean failure.

While sitting for a diploma examination, I made so many mistakes which I corrected before the exam was over. I did not fail my diploma examinations because I made mistakes. In fact, I scored the highest marks in the class. If there were to be no mistakes, then God would not have provided us with power.

Make your house a home for your family. A home is where you can find peace, joy and comfort, away from all the bombardments of the world. Parents must be patient with each other and also with their children. Parents must teach their children to do things correctly and teach them all the things they will need for survival in the future. Parents must transfer to their children all the skills they will need for life and godliness — skills for family life, for effective profit-oriented work. Children, no matter how old, need to be continually coached on how to gather wisdom, insight and understanding until they catch the vision of seeking these qualities for themselves.

We must stop drumming inferiority and mediocrity into the heads of our children. As often as you tell your child that he is stupid, useless and foolish, good for nothing, dull and a failure, his brain stores these things and he involuntarily behaves that way. So why not just bless him with good words and see him grow up into a well-organized person.

If our children are to be better problem-solvers, we must help them cultivate some stronger attitudes. They must understand that problems are not necessarily bad or abnormal — they are just a part of life. Problems can be solved peacefully, without violence. They can be solved if we are willing to work them out. We must not try to escape problems or difficulties but face them purposefully. He who fights and runs, lives to fight another day. So it is more mature to fight our problems to the end. To solve problems, we must not pretend that they are not there. If you have a problem, no amount of faith can change the fact that you have a problem. So we are better off identifying the problem, then giving the problem the attention and labor it requires to solve it. Select the closest solution to your problem. If the solution works, praise God. If it doesn't, do some strong thinking again and find a way out.

The solution to Moses' problem with how to cross the Red Sea, with the enemy advancing, was in his hand all along, but he did not know it. He needed a revelation of it.

As soon as he realized that what he needed to divide the sea was in his hand, he obeyed God and stretched forth the rod. As a result, the sea was divided. We tend to run away from problems because we convince ourselves that the solution is so big, unattainable, or far away. The answer you need is right there with you, and it is not necessarily big or far away.

We must teach our children to hold the right values and competencies. A man is not black because he was cursed when Ham was cursed, but because God made him black. A man must not be poor because he is black. A man is not any less a human being because he is black. A man is not wicked because he is white, nor is he a racist because he is white. Let's teach the future generation the right values.

Our children must have strong, Biblical values as they move into an exciting but unstable future. They must also be competent with the kind of character and maturity that does not break down or fail under stress or pressure.

Start to teach them great values early in life. It is never too late to start. Transfer to them right principles and concepts concerning others, the world, Satan, God and eternity.

We live in a time and generation when images rate higher than character, when style counts more than real accomplishments. We are impressed with outward appearances. We are easily distracted from unspectacular disciplines that lead to excellence. Life is skimmed from the surface. The depths remain largely unexplored. Parents must be committed and caring towards their children.

To be a successful parent, you must have a goal for life. You must manage your time, home, money, life and affairs well. Escapists do not get credits. Those who live responsible family lives in the arena of marriage will receive the "crown" of marriage. Your life must be well-planned so your children can see and feel its impact. Only then can you succeed in helping to plan out your children's lives. A father is a leader. In planning your life, you will definitely have to live by rules or principles. Lead your children by example.

Spend more time with your family. Read the Bible and other good books regularly. Spend at least twenty minutes praying for all your family members daily and hold family devotions with them daily. A man who fails to hold devotions with his family is laying a foundation for divorce or for a scattered family. Do more outdoor things with your children. Our children must learn from us how to be better leaders, have stronger self-esteem, know how to share problems more creatively, learn responsible work and health habits, know how to cope with guilt and how to enjoy life more abundantly.

You can also teach your children by giving them good attention. Teach them how to live a balanced Christian life as they grow up. Teach them how to analyze situations and brainstorm for solutions. Children are living, growing, changing human beings. Do not compromise the basic things of life. Be understanding and available, but do not give in to doing wrong things with your children. You may need to give them the rod occasionally. It does not matter what the social welfare people say. The Bible says to spare the rod and spoil the child. Do not abuse them, but speak to them and discipline them when they do wrong.

Teach your children how to make decisions by first teaching them how to identify the decision to be made, selecting the best options and accepting and assessing the consequences. With every opportunity, encourage your children when they are on the right track. Communicate your expectations to them. Show gratitude to them for favors done for you. Teach them how to work together in helping one another. Learn to accept your children as they are, while teaching them patiently how to change to more positive lifestyles.

You must study your child to know how to help him. Knowing your child includes discovering what makes your child angry, who his heroes are and why, what his fears are, what nicknames they call your child in school or among his peers, what are your child's favorite books, what person outside your family influences your child the most, how and where your child loves spending most of his time, what embarrasses your child and why, what would your child like most from you and what is your child's most prized possession.

The father, as a chief leader of the children, and his wife must sit down and talk about their goals as parents. Tell your wife what things you desire most that she change. Make every effort to help your wife function well in her role as a mother. You must both agree on the standards and procedures of handling your family. If you don't agree in all areas, your children will explore these disagreements to bring division. Show love for one another in front of your children.

A good father gives quality time to his family and does not waste away his time in aimless drifting of nothingness. He is consistent in all he does. His yes is yes and his no is no. He also keeps his excitement up. When the family notices that Dad has lost his enthusiasm or excitement, the family loses hope, becomes weak and cracks to the bed of darkness, gloom and sorrow.

Hard Work

A lot of smart, strong, energetic people are full of talk without action. Committees hold meetings and pass decisions but fail to properly execute such decisions. They are victims of the doldrums of inactivity. They talk and talk with no results, since no one worked for the results to follow.

Don't team up with big-mouthed people who will give you big talk, but all of it is like a noisy gong, sounding sweet but empty of results. They give all kinds of empty promises.

If a man tells you that he has succeeded before or is going to succeed and you can't see him working towards succeeding, leave him alone. If a man makes any promises to you, look to see if he can deliver the goods. What is his history like? Has he achieved his goals before? Is there fruit to substantiate his success? The Bible says, *"A man's gift maketh room for him..."* (Proverbs 18:16 KJV). A Hausa proverb says, "If someone promises you a coat, look at the one he is wearing, and do not expect anything better."

Some people assume that life can be taken on a platter of gold, and they hope to achieve abundance. They expect to wake up one day and discover that they have suddenly become rich. They hope a fortune will fall on their shoulders one day. Look at your world. There is no rich man who became a rich man without hard work. He either poured a lot of physical or mental energy into his work, or he paid others to do so for him. Lazy people always end up poor and remain poor. Poverty comes quickly to those who relax or wait for things to happen.

To be a successful man requires a lot of hard work. Some people want to get to heaven, but they do not want to do anything about getting there. They want to be great men of God, but they do not want to put any effort into it or lose any sleep. They want to be prayer warriors, but they do not want to pray. They want to be champions, but they are running away from battles and wars. Nothing good comes easy. If you want to be a successful person, you must be determined, roll up your sleeves and go to work.

I have heard people say, when one fails in other areas of life, they run into preaching, which makes preaching sound like a cheap thing to do or a cowardly choice of lifestyle. But friend, I have discovered experientially that preaching is no coward's job.

It takes all the creative ability a man can put together to work for God, especially since your Boss is invisible, and you have to discern what His plan is. He leaves you to discover the creative force and ability He planted in you. Mathematics and chemistry work on formulas, but not preaching. You have no numbers or formulas to use to get results in preaching. Only obedience to the Word of God.

Commerce depends on cash, but not preaching. All the parties involved in Gospel work are spiritual and therefore can't be seen with the physical eye. It takes a man of great mental and spiritual power to work for God. I did not say it takes an intelligent, educated man, but a man with guts. This man may be small, weak and insignificant, but he can work and satisfy an unseen Boss.

Sometimes I wish there was a formula to use to get God to do some things, so once these numbers are put together, God just has to supply the desired results. But it does not work that way. You must apply yourself to it. Pushovers who are looking for handouts never survive preaching work or the real world of honorable people.

Some people always avoid things that will give them headaches or difficulties. They want it easy. But friend, when something comes easy, it will also go easy. Difficulties only help a man develop his creative potential. Put a man in a straight jacket, and immediately he starts creating a means of getting out.

Throw a man into a pit full of snakes and see how high he will pole-vault himself out without any support or help. Those who are in a box, tight corners, and have refused to think creatively are like a dead person. They give up the determination to live. Their fighting spirit has been snuffed out.

It was hard work that built the house you live in. Have you ever thought of the volume of energy and the number of people it took to put your house together? Each time you look at your home, remember hard work. When you ride on asphalt roads and over bridges, what comes to your mind? It took many machines and men much labor to make your road smooth. You may think it was easy to build the road. But it might have taken two or three years of people's valuable, precious time and energy to bring it to a perfect state.

Desire to do hard work, for it sharpens your creative eye and ability. Stop sitting down and praying only. Step up and take action about your prayer and see what God will do.

Stop loafing. Be about the Father's business. Sleep it, walk it, talk it. Peanut oil does not come out of peanuts until you press them. The pyramids of Egypt were built with the oil pressed out of the children of Israel. When you look at the pyramids today, they are so imposing, captivating and beautiful, you don't remember, see or feel the labor put into them. I hear people talk of their inability to do certain things. For instance, music and singing. Someone says, "I can't sing." Every man can sing well if he is trained to do so. In fact, you do not know what you can do until you try. You have treasures and talents hidden within you. But cowardice will keep you from trying anything.

Some people do not want to be responsible. They are afraid of being pointed at as the cause of some bad happening, so they lose their sense of responsibility. You must take a stand. Be a person of principle. If it works or fails, be ready to take the blame or praise for it. Don't take hard work lightly. Nothing good comes easy. Lazy people lose valuable opportunities. If you must get the vitamin C that comes from oranges, you must be ready to squeeze and suck the orange, or employ someone else to get the juice out for you. Even nature works hard to put the clouds together to form water vapours before the rains fall. Your salvation did not come cheap. You were bought at an expensive price. It took hard work of reasoning and imagination for God to put all the universe and galaxies together, and finally release His only begotten Son to die for an unholy people.

No good preaching comes out of cheap effort except if it is copied from another. No music composition and production come easy. Ask someone who has done music recording. When a man attends a beautiful music concert or a well-organized power crusade, he is arrested by the glamor of the occasion, but seems to be oblivious of the hard work, meetings, sleepless nights, finances and frustrations that were at work in the background before the program came to be. If you desire to amount to something in life, then plan for some hard work.

The deliverance of the children of Israel from Egypt took Moses some strenuous blows to accomplish. People say Abraham was very rich. But he was a very hard-working man. To recruit and train shepherds into successful herdsmen and to manage the affairs of a large group of cattle and people was no joke. The disciples turned their world upside down by hard work and through the power of the Holy Ghost.

Adam and Eve were put in the garden, not to just wander around and eat fruit. They were to manage the affairs of the animal kingdom. They were to till and tend the ground. They were to trim and maintain the beautiful plants of the garden. They were expected to do some serious work to be involved with God in keeping alive His creative dream. No wonder God told them, *"And the Lord God took the man and put him in the Garden of Eden to tend and to guard and keep it"* (Genesis 2:15).

Man's duty was to cultivate and preserve the garden from all intruders. To *keep*, as used in this verse, means to hedge about and protect. The devil had already fallen, but God was aware that the devil would try to intrude, so man, apart from cultivating the garden, was to be the day and night watchman for God's newly restored garden. To guard the garden was no easy job. It called for vigilance, commitment, total persuasion and involvement. It meant giving one's life for property under his custody. Hard work will demand all these qualities from you.

Paul, in recognition of the need to work, commanded:

> *"For even when we were with you, this we commanded you, that if any would not work, neither should he eat"* (2 Thessalonians 3:10 KJV).

Idleness is a curse, and it is wrong to support men who will not work and assume their responsibility to humanity. Some people believe that carrying of briefcases from one office to the other looking for contracts is business. I call that idleness and loafing.

Sit down somewhere and find some work to do with your hands and earn some respect. Produce something and sell it to raise support for yourself and the Gospel. It does not take too much capital to do some small but good things. You don't have to start by manufacturing Rolls Royce cars or computers. Those are heavy capital investment projects. Start with something that is gainful that you can afford. Little by little, it will become something great, and you will become an employer. Don't start your business with debt. Start by using what you have, and you will be amazed how the small five loaves and two fishes will be turned to millions of loaves and fishes until you cannot consume it all.

Paul worked with his hands, and he did not borrow. He was not chargeable to any man. He worked night and day so he wouldn't be dependent upon others for support. No wonder Paul could say:

> *"...for we behaved not ourselves disorderly among you; Neither did we eat any man's bread for nought; but wrought with labor and travail night and day, that we might not be chargeable to any of you"* (2 Thessalonians 3:7-8 KJV).

Don't tell me you cannot find a job to do. You can chart your course in the world of business by inventing some work for yourself. Do not be busy about useless matters. Some people are doing everything they should not do. They meddle in the business of others, preying into the domestic affairs of others. Such people are a curse to any neighborhood and a plague to every religious group.

Stop doing too many things or thinking of too many things at the same time. Jesus visited Mary and Martha and sat down to teach. Mary sat with Him, but Martha went to look for firewood, fetch water and make some fire to cook food for Jesus. That sounds very noble, but it wasn't as good as sitting down at the Master's feet to eat the Bread of Life. Martha was overwhelmed by her many cooking plans and projects, so she asked Jesus to rebuke Mary and have her help with the cooking. Jesus said, *"...Martha, Martha, thou art careful and troubled about many things: But one thing is needful: and Mary hath chosen that good part..."* (Luke 10:41-42 KJV).

Don't try to get into too many things at the same time. You can be in only one place at a time. Many people join too many groups and associations, and at the end are rendered ineffective and useless. Don't be jack of all trades and master of none. Man has the capacity to handle only one thing effectively at a given time. Don't give your business to a master of all trades to handle. Too many cooks spoil the broth. Too many commitments to practical ideas make a man mad. For he will be tossed about like the waves or the winds of the sea. He will be unsteady and unfruitful.

Years ago I was in a meeting when someone prophesied over me a most magnificent prophecy. At the end, he looked at me and said, "Son, if you don't water this word with your actions, labor and prayers, it will die just as a seed dies in the soil if it is not supplied with water." Some of us are clinging to projects or courses that have long died. We are looking up expectantly. We have become so busy expecting that we have no time for corresponding action and watering of the Word. We pray but there are no results, no answers. We conclude that God does not answer prayer, but God answered long ago when He sent the manna into the wilderness. We must go and carry it ourselves. He will not throw it into our mouth. We must get out there and ask, seek and even knock. Add action to your prayers, and you will see a difference.

A young man building a ministry kept believing God and confessing for numerical growth and development. All he did was pray, fast and go out to look for money. He failed to put the appropriate corresponding action to his prayers and fasting. Faith without works is dead. Many visions are aborted because of a lack of corresponding action.

So we must labor on with the dream. We must water, cultivate and guard it to see fruit. Don't just pray "Thy kingdom come," but add action to it, and you will see His will and Kingdom spread.

One old writer wrote this song:

**When the trumpet of the Lord shall sound and time
shall be no more.
And the morning breaks, eternal bright and fair,
When the saved on earth shall gather over on the other
shore.
And the roll is called up yonder I'll be there.**

**When the roll is called up yonder,
When the roll is called up yonder,
When the roll is called up yonder,
When the roll is called up yonder I'll be there.**

**On that bright and cloudless morning
When the dead in Christ shall rise
And the glory of His resurrection share
When His chosen ones shall gather
To their homes beyond the skies
And the roll is called up yonder I'll be there.**

**Let us labor for the Master from the dawn till setting
sun
Let us tell of His wondrous love and care,
Then when all of life is over and our work on earth is
done
And the roll is called up yonder I'll be there.**

If we want to see blessing on our work and vision, we must discover and release the appropriate corresponding actions and labor for the Master.

The hard work of Nehemiah earned him a place in the holy Scriptures. He left an example worthy of emulating. He and his men attacked the rebuilding of the holy walls with a special zeal. They hardly had time for food, let alone time to change their clothes or shoes. No one really cared about how he looked or felt. The most conscious thing was the work at hand.

*"Those who built the wall and those who bore burdens
loaded themselves so that everyone worked with one hand
and held a weapon with the other hand. And every builder*

had his sword girded by his side, and so worked. And he who sounded the trumpet was at my side.

*"So we **labored at the work** while half of them held the spears from **dawn until the stars came out**.*

"So none of us — I, my kinsmen, my servants, nor the men of the guard who followed me —took off our clothes; each kept his weapon [in his hand for days]" (Nehemiah 4:17,18,21,23).

A hard working man is a treasure! Who can find one so easily?

"He becometh poor that dealeth with a slack [idle] hand: but the hand of the diligent maketh rich" (Proverbs 10:4 KJV).

"The slothful (lazy) man does not catch his game or roast it once he kills it, but the diligent man gets precious possessions" (Proverbs 12:27).

"The thoughts of the [steadily] diligent tend only to plenteousness, but everyone who is impatient and hasty hastens only to want" (Proverbs 21:5).

"Do you see a man diligent and skillful in his business? He will stand before kings; he will not stand before obscure men" (Proverbs 22:29).

Now let's talk about this. What is *diligence*? It means a steady, earnest and energetic application of effort towards a goal. A diligent man painstakingly applies himself to his vision. He studies his job or vision. He knows his facts well. He knows what it takes and how to apply himself well so minimum effort brings out a good yield. He is so proficient in his work that when you give him a work to do, you are restful about it, because you know the result will be perfect.

"Be diligent to know the state of your flocks, and look well to your herds" (Proverbs 27:23).

Analyze your work structure so that you can develop the science of effective work performance.

Have you ever seen a man who lost his last penny? He will leave no stone unturned in his effort to find that coin.

He will climb all the climbable places. He will enter all holes just to find that penny. If your vision or business were that penny, I am sure all non-essential issues of life that are keeping you from advancing would have been moved aside long ago. Because that coin is so important, you will stop at nothing to find it.

> *"Or what woman, having ten [silver] drachmas [each one equal to a day's wage], if she loses one coin, does not light a lamp and sweep the house and look carefully and diligently until she finds it?* (Luke 15:8).

So many people fail to progress in life because they refuse to light up their lamps by putting truth, purity, sincerity and honesty into their day-by-day existence. They refuse to sweep out all the cobwebs that have held them bound. They must sweep out trickery and corruption, fear and discouragement. Except this is done, success will necessarily elude them and their efforts will be useless since their fruit will not abide or endure.

Do It Over Again

Stick to your efforts stubbornly. Do not let past failures taunt you. Refuse to remember them except to learn from them in a positive way.

When Peter walked on the water, he did not initially fear failure, until he saw the boisterous wind. When Jesus held Peter from drowning, they walked back together on the water with Jesus to the boat. Peter did not try it again.

When God told Noah to build a boat, he was not full of fear of failure. He knew God had spoken and given him a blueprint that would work. When God gives you a blueprint, step out boldly and blow the trumpet. Our main problem is not being able to make a discovery or find a blueprint. But our main problem is to find God. Once we find Him, He will give us a blueprint.

When you achieve success, note the scheme or key used and repeat it again. Don't stop using that key. When you play the guitar and find the right key combination for a song,

you don't keep searching for more keys, but you keep playing those keys. If a drummer is playing a song, he does not
keep changing his drum style, he keeps playing the same
style until the song comes to an end.

Many people are quick in giving up keys or principles
they have found, in search of new ones, and they lose even
the little success they have achieved. Don't stop using your
key to success until you find a more excellent one.

Reverence

Some people who have been destined to be millionaires
have remained "thousandaires" simply because they do not
have the fear of God in them. They have no time for God.
They believe that they are the "be alls" and "do alls." They
believe that their world of success starts and ends with them
and their intelligence. They may hypocritically claim to be
thanking God, but in their heart they believe they do not
need God.

> "For who separates you from the others [as a fac-
> tion leader]? [Who makes you superior and sets you
> apart from another, giving you the preeminence?] What
> have you that was not given to you? If then you re-
> ceived it [from someone], why do you boast as if you
> had not received [but had gained it by your own ef-
> forts]?

> "[You behave as if] you are already filled and think
> you have enough [you are full and content, feeling no
> need of anything more]! Already you have become rich
> [in spiritual gifts and graces]! [Without any counsel or
> instruction from us, in your conceit], you have ascended
> your thrones and come into your kingdom without
> including us!" (1 Corinthians 4:7,8).

Success has an evil, which is big-headedness, treating
people and the things of God lightly. Treating people as
though they were only things to be used. For one to have
good success, he must learn to revere God. He must learn
to honor God. It is more difficult to handle success than

failure. *"...For those who honor Me I will honor, and those who despise Me shall be lightly esteemed"* (1 Samuel 2:30).

Search history and you will find that all who revered God were rich, enjoyed their wealth and increased abundantly. But those who despised God disappeared suddenly and ended up amounting to nothing, like the flower of the field that dies and is burned with fire.

Tracing through the lineages of Karl Marx, the socialist, about 100 people from his generation to the present were studied. Out of these 100 people, only one person ever amounted to anything. The rest were riff-raffs, nonachievers and non-entities. All died poor and wretched. The only one who amounted to something was interestingly a strongly committed child of God.

On the other hand, D. L. Moody, a man who feared God to the core, was also studied. Out of 100 family members from his generation until now, 99 per cent of them ended up as successful engineers, doctors, lawyers, pastors and many other professions, and only one man ended up amounting to nothing in life. What a great difference! It must be great to fear God. You see, your success is useless until your descendants end up blessed. The only way to guarantee that is to be full of reverence for God.

Many people are anointed for business, to make money, anointed to preach or pray, etc., but people rarely are anointed to fear God. Also, they rarely are anointed to hear from the Spirit or are anointed to be thoughtful, sober, calm and collected. Many do not even find the need to walk in the Spirit. The fear of God is the beginning of wisdom. We exhibit our lack of fear in the way we treat our prayer meetings and neglect our personal prayers and Bible reading. We show our gross disinterest in God when we enter His sanctuary. We show no respect whatsoever. In church or fellowship, we walk about when a meeting is in progress. We forget that we came for a meeting with the Most High and He demands our utmost respect. Who in the world will go to visit his head of state and keep walking all around backing him as they walk?

> *"You shall keep My Sabbaths and* **reverence** *My sanctuary. I am the Lord"* (Leviticus 19:30).

We do not find it interesting to giggle and do some side talking until we come to meetings in the house of the Lord. Then we stand around in talk-show groups while the meeting is in progress, and God is trying to talk to us. In fact, at such times, God has to struggle to get our attention. The way we treat God in the sanctuary shows how much respect we attach to Him in our private lives.

Some of us are so used to God that we treat Him like a house boy! No matter how close we are with God, God is still God, and we should stand in awe of His power. Avoid familiarity with God, the things of God, or men of God. Familiarity breeds contempt. And contempt hatches rebellion and stubbornness. Stubbornness and rebellion are as the sin of witchcraft (1 Samuel 15:23). *"Thou shalt not suffer a witch to live"* (Exodus 22:18 KJV).

> *"Let us therefore, receiving a kingdom that is firm and stable and cannot be shaken, offer to God pleasing service and acceptable worship, with modesty and pious care and godly fear and awe; For our God [is indeed] a consuming fire"* (Hebrews 12:28-29).

We must stop handling God's affairs as we would handle a carnal business. We must stop handling God carelessly or craftily.

> *"Keep your foot [give your mind to what you are doing] when you go [as Jacob to sacred Bethel] to the house of God. For to draw near to hear and obey is better than to give the sacrifice of fools [carelessly, irreleventy] too ignorant to know that they are doing evil.*
>
> *"Be not rash with your mouth, and let not your heart be hasty to utter a word before God. For God is in heaven, and you are on earth; therefore let your words be few"* (Ecclesiastes 5:1,2).

To treat God irreverently will earn us some chastisement. Saul treated God irreverently. God stripped him of his property and crown.

> *"Samuel said, Has the Lord as great a delight in burnt offerings and sacrifices as in obeying the voice of the Lord? Behold, to obey is better than sacrifice, and to hearken than the fat of rams. For rebellion is as the sin of witchcraft, and stubbornness is as idolatry...Because you have rejected the word of the Lord, He also has rejected you from being king. And Saul said to Samuel, I have sinned; for I have transgressed the commandment of the Lord and your words, because I feared the people and obeyed their voice"* (1 Samuel 15:22-24).

Saul disregarded God's words. He treated them as though they were Samuel's words. He repented later, but God could not change His mind, for He does not repent as the sons of men do. Saul offered the sacrifices of fools. He thought that if he could do a show with Agag the king, the sheep, rams and goats, God would be pleased. He thought God was interested in sacrifices, so he spared Agag and offered burnt offerings to God from the booty. God would surely be impressed, he thought. Little did he know that he was reasoning as a fool and offering the sacrifices of fools.

> *"Hear, O my people, and I will speak; O Israel, I will testify to you and against you: I am God, your God. I do not reprove you for your sacrifices; your burnt offerings are continually before Me. I will accept no bull from your house nor he-goat out of your folds. For every beast of the forest is Mine, and the cattle upon a thousand hills or upon the mountains where thousands are.*
>
> *"I know and am acquainted with all the birds of the mountains, and the wild animals of the field are Mine and are with Me, and in My mind. If I were hungry, I would not tell you, for the world and its fullness are Mine. Shall I eat the flesh of bulls or drink the blood of goats?*
>
> *"Offer to God the sacrifice of thanksgiving, and pay your vows to the Most High. And call on Me in the day of*

trouble; I will deliver you, and you shall honor and glorify Me" (Psalm 50:7-15).

A fool thinks that God is interested in his money or other material substances. He fails to realize that God owns all things. He takes a little out of his abundance and gives to God in a public show and expects God to say thank you. But he fails to note that God sees the plenty hidden away from the eyes of the public. He receives praise for all good deeds shown and claims to be humble, but fails to realize that God knows the secret condition (pride) of his heart.

"For I desire and delight in dutiful steadfast love and goodness, not sacrifice, and the knowledge of and acquaintance with God more than burnt offerings" (Hosea 6:6).

"And if you had only known what this saying means, I desire mercy [readiness to help, to spare, to forgive] rather than sacrifice and sacrificial victims..." (Matthew 12:7).

God desires men who will fear Him in their public lives and in their private, secret lives — from their utterances to the thought of their hearts and minds. If He finds such a one, He will endue him with divine, creative revelations, be they in business or ministry.

Stop walking in and out of prayer meetings. Stop making passes, idle talk, or pass signs to each other during intercession. God is real, and He gets offended with such irreverences.

Get a Flaming Desire

To succeed, you need a strong desire. Indifference and a lackadaisical attitude will only lead you into deep poverty and slow death. A strong desire is your point of departure. A definite desire produces results. We cannot afford to think in generalities. Wishing and desire are not friends. Wish is a failure graduate, but desire is a friend of victors and conquerors. When you get a red hot desire, you turn on the power of drive. It is this power of drive or urge that leads to achievements.

If one desires a thing strong enough and seeks it with all his heart, he is bound to succeed. There will be no stopping him. Stop being a spectator. Instead, catch a flaming desire and make history. Stop desiring only your corner and explore the world of possibilities. Attempt something new, something extraordinary. Press unto the end of the efforts of your desires. Switch fully to the high beam. Be ready to make the supreme sacrifice needed to prosper your desires.

As you take your leap into the promised land of your desires, "doctors" of caution on risks and brave ideas will warn you, "Don't work too hard, use your head or save a little for a rainy day and don't give too much." They will say, "Be careful. Don't do that. Take it easy, lest you break down." Or they will say, "Don't invest now, there are too many hazards. What if you fail?" Or, "I have tried that and failed. Conditions are hopeless. Let's wait until tomorrow."

Stay away from these caution experts. Avoid such worries and negatives like the bubonic plague. Live in expectancy. If you have a desire, you are a pregnant person. All pregnant women are expectant people. Invest in the future. Don't be afraid of trying, and stop putting yourself in the security zone. All who play it safe never arrive in their promised land. Do not be content with your small world. Move into the large society of great dreamers.

The world is so wide that there are pyramids of opportunities still looking for people to discover them. So let the flames of fire catch you, nourish your desire so that it will not fade away. Desire your goal strong enough. Feed it to grow and develop by constantly working on it. If any yearning in your heart does not grow and develop, it will disintegrate and disappear, leaving only emptiness, unconcern and indifference in your vision. So put that desire to use, ponder it, develop it and cause it to grow.

Develop a strong will and determination to realize your goal. Search for ways of doing so. The shepherds were told of the Savior's birth. God did not pick them up and throw them in the manger, though He had the power to do so. They had to use their strong desire to find Christ, so they earnestly sought for Him until they found Him. Life is for seeking. Do not wait for your dream to walk into your house. Work it out. Every man is a success if he works at it and keeps his will to do so on fire.

> "That you may walk (live and conduct yourselves) in a manner worthy of the Lord, fully pleasing to Him and desiring to please Him in all things, bearing fruit in every good work..." (Colossians 1:10).

Cherish Your Own Individuality

We are unique. We are incomprehensible. No two of us are alike. We must know our unique potential, develop our personalities, and intensify and dignify it. Conformity is a crime. We must explore and use our personalities and contribute our distinctness to the larger community. Don't underestimate yourself, you are a bundle of potential. A man is only as small or as big as he thinks. "For as he thinks in his heart, so is he..." (Proverbs 23:7).

Employ self-examination, self-scrutiny and self-analysis to know yourself. Examine your values. Discover your hidden talents. Know how far you have used them. Rate yourself and move into greater use of what you have. Develop confidence in God's ability planted within you. There are things in life that no one will help you conquer. You must conquer them alone. No man should need another to be able to walk around unless he is ill. Likewise, you will have to help yourself because no one else will. Accept yourself as you are, and enjoy living with yourself.

Many people are victims of self-degradation, self-criticism and defacing of self-ability. They call themselves ants and earthworms. They believe they are good for nothing. But if the Almighty God dwells in you, you are now good for every situation. I am not encouraging you to trust in yourself or push high your evil ego. Of a truth, people who hold themselves in low esteem find it necessarily hard to succeed in life. Men, you are the best. You stand greater chances of succeeding than anyone else in your situation. You alone can perform your function best. You alone know your road in life best.

You need self-acceptance, not self-rejection. Do not be ashamed because you are not meeting up with people's expectations. Refuse to be full of despair over your inadequacies. Instead, seek for ways to triumph over them.

Do not accuse yourself, lest you start hating yourself and others. Learn from failure and move on to victory. Appreciate and respect yourself, and others will, too. Sow self-respect and you will receive respect from others. If you aren't succeeding now, do not hate or reject the successful life, but be full of appreciation for the success in another. Know what you stand for and whom you represent.

The making of a successful man is a process. No man is born ready-made. God knew that ready-made people will not fit into life. Life will tear such people into shreds, so He made man to grow into his dreams. Therefore, it is now up to us to grow into winning or losing. As you face crisis after crisis, you will become a winner, a conqueror.

The world will not be a successful place if individuals do not succeed. Therefore, make your contribution toward world betterment. Creative individuals bring progress into the world. Search yourself, find out what your purpose in life is. Find your station. Develop into an achiever. Do not be a passive onlooker as others pass you on their way to self-development and enlargement.

It is up to you to be somebody in this life. Nobody will make you but you. No wonder the Bible says, *"A man's gift makes room for him..."* (Proverbs 18:16).

Be what you are, and be it to the fullest. That will lead to greater spheres where you can be what you ought to be. It is hard to ask a pig to get out of the pit and go to the palace. So don't expect yourself to be what you can't be right now. Be what you can be. Be what you really are to the fullest. Do not expect to start driving a Rolls Royce when you can't afford a bicycle. You must crawl before you walk and run.

So begin to build your life on what you have and on where you are right now. Face problems with boldness, simply because you know the Problem-Solver!

For What Will You Be Remembered?

When your name is mentioned in the future after you have left this life, for what will you be remembered?

Many people have successfully labored in various fields of human endeavor. Some are known for their miraculous discoveries, and others for their creative abilities in the field of medicine, agriculture, electronics, aviation, etc. What are you going to be known for? Or, what are you planning to be known for? Some people are known for their great evils and destructiveness. Records can be broken, positively or negatively. A good man is known for his many good deeds. And a thief is known by his many evil exploits. The wicked shall not stand in the judgment, nor the sinners in the congregation of right-standing people.

Many people will be remembered for their great contributions to life. Some will be remembered as engineers, physicians, preachers, justices, or politicians. They created ways where there were no ways. They had the ability to overcome discouragement and failure. For what will you be remembered? With God's help, try to set a record, a mark by which the world can remember you. Leave a landmark and a testimony for yourself.

Mockery

When people mock you, realize that you must be doing something right. Something progressive must be happening. No one in good health will mock and scoff at a leper, because the leper has nothing that a man in good health would be jealous or envious of. In the same way, a rich man has no business being jealous or envious of a poor man. The sun cannot be jealous of darkness. The man who is above cannot be envious of the man beneath. The superior cannot be jealous or envious of the inferior. If men are mocking you, know that you are above and you are heading for a better place than they. Your progress is provoking them to jealousy. One of the signs of a winner is that people may be jealous of him and therefore resort to mockery.

Nehemiah was doing a good job building the wall of Jerusalem. Apparently, their enemies could not understand the courage and determination of these zealots. Therefore, they tried to get the king to stop them, but when that failed and Nehemiah obviously was succeeding, they resorted to mockery.

As soon as you hit success, faultfinders will bring out their microscopes and begin to look for faults. They will point four accusing fingers at you. They will rub your nose on the ground until you can take it no more. They want you to join them in the non-achievers discouragement club. They want you to sit in the mud with them and sing by the rivers of Babylon. If you dare to waste your time challenging them, you will have no time attending to the business of success at hand. You must realize that storms must be challenged with greater zeal and effort. Let the storms make you rise higher like the eagle rather than discourage you. Use mockery as a stepping-stone to your promised land rather than knock you off course. Let the mockery keep you on the forward march instead of at a standstill.

Isaac got so prosperous that the Philistines envied him. They had no right to be envious, but they were. They plugged the well that his father's servants had dug. Isaac did not give up hope but dug another group of wells, and instead of finding water, he found springing wells. What a lesson! If the mocker and the devil spoil your chances, dig another well! Knock at another door, and you will find springing waters. If a community refuses to accept you, move on into the next community. Your springing wells may be located there. Those who rejected you simply helped you to find your wells of springing waters. Don't waste your time with accusers, faultfinders and compromisers. Keep your distance from them, but if they identify anything you are doing wrong, correct it, apologize for it and keep working toward success. Do not look back after you have put your hand on the plough (Luke 9:62).

> *"And the man* [Isaac] *became great and gained more and more until he became very wealthy and distinguished; He owned flocks, herds, and a great supply of servants, and the Philistines envied him. Now all the wells which his father's servants had dug in the days of Abraham his father, the Philistines had closed and filled with earth...Now Isaac's servants dug in the valley and found a well of living [spring] water..."* (Genesis 26:13-15,19).

It is in the valley of the shadow of death that you will find your springing wells.

Who told you the valley of the shadow of death was entirely useless? Isaac proved that anyone who cares and dares to check the valley will find springs of living waters, or gold of great value. Do not get burned up when fire is set under you. Get refined and recharged!

12
Diabolical Plots

There is a lot of deceit in existence to-day all around us. If you have not been caught in the web of these tricksters and hooksters, your brother or someone living next to you has. Because of the escalation of stress and stress-related problems, people are desperately running to and fro looking for some lasting, potent form of relief. In this condition, many people have dabbled in the occult or occult-related activities.

Our generation, more than any other before us, has witnessed an unprecedented increase of interest in the psychic phenomenon. Along with this comes the dabbling into Eastern mystic religions. In this same category falls the deceptive, unrealistic promises of the Middle East Arabic superstitious religion of Islam, which comes to a home to separate brother from brother and parents from children. It promises to make its captives better human beings to the unconverted. It promises to free people from burdens it hardly understands. It shouts, "Peace, peace," but it brings confusion into families, groups and nations. The more the confusion, the better Islam thrives. It operates best by setting people against one another, even within the mosque and sets Moslems against themselves. It promises brotherly love, but instead, it teaches its adherents to hate anyone not related to Islam by conversion.

Islam may be handing out food, clothing and shelter to the needy, but it also enlists them into the most bitter, violent aggressive racists, terrorists and wicked, vicious human life hunters the world has ever known. Islam promises to provide solutions to the problems of the world, especially racism and oppression, but in reality, all it does is hit the most affected at their weakest point and greatest area of need to gather cheap converts. It then teaches the converts that anyone who does not believe like they do is not fit to live. Such are either to be converted or exterminated at the slightest provocation.

Unfortunately, many well-meaning people with sincere motives to sanitize the world and create equality among all races and classes, have been overtaken by this deception and false, endless promises. They have been convinced by great swelling words of promises of liberty from oppressors. Instead of liberty from oppressors, they have been venomized against other races or people of a different social class. They become victims of what they were to heal. If a doctor is sick, it is difficult to help another sick person. A dead man cannot come to the aid of another dead person, no matter how close he lies to him.

My desire in this piece of inspired literature is to reveal to all who care to know, the deep secrets of unravelled wickedness, deceit and hypocrisy locked in and stored up in Islam.

In all my years of traveling all over the world, I have been struck most by the way people in Europe, America and elsewhere are being cheaply sweet-tongued into joining Islam. In America it promises the American Africans freedom from their white "oppressors." In Europe it promises youths freedom from the moral and social limitations Christianity places over them. In Africa it promises protection, power and wealth to her greedy national leaders. To their poor it promises instant wealth from the blessings of Allah and total eradication of poverty and its related, numerous problems. In Asia it promises arms to those struggling to free themselves of some tribal, regional, or ethnic bondage.

The typical Moslem "evangelist" is an opportunist. He has keen eyes to catch the heartbeat of a society, diagnose the weakest or most needy group and promise the fulfillment of its desires. He promises to team up with such groups to fight the oppressor, even within families. They study it and approach such a one with some special disadvantage within the family and give promises of greatness. It almost takes an angel to reject and turn away from a man who offers you bread when you are hungry, a coat when you are cold, a drink when you are thirsty or money when you are poor. In this way many have fallen into the dangerous contract of selling their souls to a religion that has no salvation plan. Islam is totally based on rumors and hearsay. Its founder, Mohammed, had no definite assurance at his death and could only console his fanatics with the advice that everyone should seek the best way to his own god.

Having been trained in my youth in the basic terms of Islam, having lived all my life in the midst of Moslems, I have watched and experienced some of the most vicious aggression, killings and maiming of human beings by so-called Moslem jihadists. Therefore, I found myself obligated and compelled to say something to those unsuspecting youths and converts being deceived into Islam.

All nations that opened their doors to Islam soon discover a great rise in terrorist activities, religious intolerance and violence, religious discrimination and wars. Lebanon is a very good example of what Islamic aggression admitted into a nation can do. Any family who gets infected by Islam through one member, invites devastating rivalry, clamor and violence into their home. It is not unbecoming to a Moslem to be taught that he has the right to take the life of his father, mother, brother or sister because they do not support Islam, and as such, are not fit to relate with the converted. He cannot be advised by his family. He cannot eat meat which was not slaughtered by him or a Moslem imam. He cannot eat food on the same plate with "Kafiri" (or infidel, anyone who is not a Moslem), even if the father of such a Moslem convert is a great Christian leader. In fact, the more involved you are with Christianity, the greater a "Kafiri" you are to a Moslem and your Moslem-converted son. Moslems have no family ties or affiliations except in the brotherhood of Islam, which doesn't even stick. They have no family or moral values.

Islam, from its past track record of violence, is a wild animal on the loose. And anyone who loves their nation will warn it about the dangers of giving Islam any form of romance or foothold, let alone a stranglehold over family, economic, or state affairs. Moslem leaders are some of the most unpredictable and unreliable people you will ever deal with. They easily say yes to you, but they really mean no. They will pretend to be your friend until they know they have possessive power over you. Then they will strike with a deadly blow.

For a long time, people have regarded communism as the greatest threat to world peace, stability and rational understanding. But communism, with her great persecution, injustice and wickedness, does not have the vast potential for violence that Islam holds. Islam strongly believes in divide and rule, or create violence, chaos and confusion between family members, tribes and nations and then rule them. Whether it is to the detriment of such converts, it does not matter as long as Islam gets a foothold.

To encourage this violent spirit and approach, it is said that if a Moslem dies in the course of fighting for Allah, he goes straight to heaven. So you have Moslems all over who live and thrive in confusion and chaotic conditions because they hope to kill others or even be killed in their fight for Allah to force the world to Islamize. The Western world does not seem to understand the frame of mind of the Moslem terrorist who hijacks a plane full of Westerners. To him he is fighting for Allah, and these hostages are nothing but a bunch of animals whose lives mean nothing to him or Allah since they are "kafiris." He would easily shoot one in the head, without the slightest feeling of guilt or remorse, because he has only helped Allah destroy one of his rivals. The terrorist cares little for his life, because he thinks to die means to be with Allah in heaven. So when you come to liberate the hostages by force, he prefers to kill all and die with them, since this is his surest ticket to a so-called blissful heaven.

America and the Western nations can no longer be neutral. This is important to realize as the planet plunges towards a vicious era of terrorism and racial and religious intolerance. Every nation, willingly or unwillingly, is involved in the racial and religious scenarios. The Arab strength is determined to force all nations to accept Islam as a worldwide force. Their aim is to conquer the world by hook or by crook. If they can't get the world by peace, they are fully determined to take it by stimulating clannish, tribal, or racial jihads. Unfortunately, the Western world is so taken by her pride in the boast of her Western powers, she under-estimates the ability of the Moslem Arabs. Either overtly or covertly, the Western world has aided the Arab Islamic colonizers to buy up businesses in the Western economic system, which will be used in the future to subjugate the West. The Arabs boast of their black gold, which they plan to use as their final joker to bring the West and America to her knees and forcefully Islamize the world which depends on her black gold.

The Arab world is without conscience or respon-sibility, so you can believe that it will mean nothing to them to starve the West of oil, which she greatly needs to run her super-industrialized lifestyle.

Seeing the Problem Correctly

The so-called Christian West and America are losing their promising youths to the deceits of the promise of riches or equality in Islam, because no one, or very few, are doing something constructive or intentional to help disadvantaged people, whether black or white. No one really cares that much in the Church about the quality of life in the church people as long as the numbers add up. We want to have the population in the church on Sunday in the thousands, and whether these people are doing well is a thing we only give a mental show of recognition and no realistic problem-solving action. The old greed rushes to have thousands in the church without plans to handle the problems and responsibilities of having a large church family. Numbers boast the ego. The church must start taking its rightful place in the lives of the youths, the needy and the helpless.

White and black churches must stop talking about black disadvantages, while Moslems are in Harlem, Brooklyn or somewhere else handing out support in tangible forms of food and housing, making cheap converts out of those the church should have helped long ago. The Church of Christ must start doing something positive. Jesus is hungry and homeless in the bodies of those needy ones sleeping under bridges and along roadsides.

What do we intend to do about it? These challenges must be faced. Black churches alone may not have the resources to help the situation. White churches must get involved. The problem is not just a black and white one, it is the Lord's burden and yoke. Shall we claim to be His disciples and fail to carry the burden He called us to carry? There is a defeatist attitude which says the situation can't be helped. The strength of the Church is being swept away by a mighty rushing circuit of sea waves. We do not need pessimists around when some people are drowning in a godless religion and are headed for a godless eternity. Needy youths can't be blamed for turning to Islam since it gives them a listening ear and a caring attitude. An understanding heart and a helping hand are attractive. It is not for the good of a drowning man to start arguing about *how* to save him. All he needs is *out!* After he gets out, then talk. True religion is not gauged by how much we speak, but by how much help we give. Jesus said:

> *"...Begone from Me, you cursed, into the eternal fire prepared for the devil and his angels! For I was hungry and you gave Me no food, I was thirsty and you gave Me nothing to drink, I was a stranger and you did not welcome Me and entertain Me, I was naked and you did not clothe Me, I was sick and in prison and you did not visit Me with help and ministering care"* (Matthew 25:41-43).

My true friend, it is not the one who studies how to help, but the one who really does help, who does something that counts for eternity.

13
Solution to Youth Drifting

Young American Africans are disappointed with the church because it talks
of love, care and tenderness, but does not
show it. It says, "God bless you, stay
warm," but closes its eyes on the real pressing needs of the people. Those in the church
must see it as their responsibility to help those who are
struggling. No one succeeds for himself alone. When God
grants you success, He does so you can help another person
succeed. When God lifts a man up, He does it so he can, in
turn, lift someone else up.

The rich man thinks of his wealth as an impregnable
defence, a high wall of safety. What a dreamer! Money has a
way of leaving people who refuse to use it to help the poor
and to help those who will use it correctly. Often, people are
limited by color when it comes to helping in the household
of God. This should not be evident among us. Can a successful white businessman help a struggling black man and
raise him up in business? Can the black man help his struggling white brother? There are not many black, wealthy
brothers, because for so long, the blacks lived wretched lives
and were subjected to grand poverty in slavery and are just
now rising up. Our white well-to-do brethren have a very
special opportunity to show some of the underprivileged
blacks simple Christian love by helping them out in business, especially where blacks are making good efforts and
showing signs of being responsible and determined to
work hard. Such struggling black men who are pressing
on to success and abundance should not be seen by their

white counterparts as competitors, but as partners in progress.

A dear friend told me how he approached a white well-to-do brother whom he thought loved him dearly and asked for a small loan to help set up a business. This white brother said he had no such money, yet the same week he gave a white young man a large sum to help him in his struggling business. This young man was well-known to my dear black friend unfortunately, so he heard where the young white man got his loan. You can imagine how he felt. The color preference had blinded the successful white man from helping the black man.

There are many examples of such discrimination. It ought not to be. I am not saying we must help people because they are black. But if the white brethren will go out of their way to show interest in the black man, it will help to reduce friction and restore confidence in the genuineness of the Gospel we believe and hold dear. The idea that Christianity is synonymous with the white man is a deception of the devil. The white man has long been identified with the Gospel. Men (and women), regardless of color, need to demonstrate the Gospel with their lifestyle.

Some churches still hold the obnoxious belief, either consciously or unconsciously, that the curse Noah placed on Ham passed down to the blacks and is still in force.

> *"When Noah awoke from his drunken stupor, and learned what had happened and what Ham, his younger son, had done, he cursed Ham's descendants: 'A curse upon the Canaanites,' he swore. 'May they be the lowest of slaves to the descendants of Shem and Japheth'"* (Genesis 9:24-25 TLB).

The people whom Noah cursed to be slaves were not all the sons of Ham. The sons of Canaan were the Canaanites who had to be flushed out of the promised land to make a place for the Israelites. This curse placed them on a danger list with God, so to speak. God gave them up for the righteous Israelites who served Him. The Cushites were not mentioned as those to share the curse, even though they were descendants of Ham.

It may be noteworthy to mention here that all colors have, at one time or another, been slaves. It only happens that the black race was among the last people to be dehumanized into slavery. God gave up the Canaanites because they were cursed and doomed to ruin, not the blacks. Apart from the Chinese and the Indians, the black race is the only group of people growing today at an alarming rate. The curse did not affect the black race.

Let's assume for a moment that the curse was on Cush, the father of the blacks, and not on Canaan, the father of the Canaanites. That curse was broken about 2,000 years ago on the cross of Calvary. It is of non-effect today. In fact, it became of no effect the very day Jesus died. When He died, He released the Cushites, the Canaanites and all races from the pre-Calvary curses. If God could annul the greatest curse of all curses, which Adam and Eve brought to the human race through sin, God will surely forgive the curse of drunken Lot. When Jesus said, *"It is finished"* on the cross, He meant all of the curse for all people groups and cultures was done away with.

Some white preachers have said, "God hates sin no more than he hates to see a black man marry a white woman." Such inflammatory statements are grossly unbecoming of an ambassador of Christ, sent to reconcile the world of all race and colors back to God. When God forbade the Jews from intermarriage with the Canaanites, He did so to keep the Canaanite women from seducing their husbands to serve Baal instead of the Lord God Almighty. But in the household of God, there is no black, white, Jew, or Greek for all who serve the Lord God Almighty. It is in the spirit of the New Testament to allow interracial marriage in Christ. Christ is the unifying factor.

I do know that integration of all races will surely take time, but we should not help the devil to delay it by our utterances, attitudes and behaviors based on ignorance of

God's Word. It is for this reason that the cause of the cross and the Gospel has been smeared. Neither whites nor blacks have any right to look down on one another. When the soul and spirit of man return to God, we will not be judged on white or black skin. We will be judged on *sin*.

We must teach our children positive attitudes toward people of other races and creeds. We should be accepting, absorbing and blind to color. Tolerance is wrong. Instead, we must accept one another honestly as we are. Only then will the world see and marvel, "See how these people love one another, even though they are of different colors, creeds and nationalities." God is standing by to give us all the necessary grace to do what is right. The potential for integration is within us. We must release it so the Gospel can truly take its proper position in the hearts of all men. Let's not, by ignorant behavior and utterances, block the positive work of the Gospel.

If the church will stop playing racial politics and the building of personal kingdoms, and start becoming involved radically with the needs of youths, whether they are white or black, a powerful revival will again return to the Church. Instead of building names and individual kingdoms, church leaders need to start building people and the Kingdom of God. Jesus is all that matters. The Kingdom is His. We are only His laborers. It is time to remove our masks and be real. The world needs to see more of the character of Christ, Who died for sinners, fed the hungry, housed the homeless, clothed the naked and visited the prisoners. The world is waiting to see more of these character traits flowing freely in and through our lives. Only then will the world come to ask what we are all about. Then we will have an opportunity to tell them that it is Jesus Who makes the difference in us.

All it takes for us to be possessed of these traits is to be real in our prayers and in our lifestyles. Then God will reveal to us our nakedness and needy state. We will stop feeling so important about ourselves and stop exalting ordinary servants. We will exalt Jesus. In this way, He will draw men to Himself. We must stop all self-promotion and carnal pride that come from our small achievements. We must stop the polished preaching, self-aggrandizement, pomposity and reckless spiritual lives. It is time for preachers to clean up their acts, straighten their roads and fix their deeds. We must make up our minds who we want to serve — race, color of the skin, money, fashions, women, lusts, names, positions, or *Christ*!

Have you ever wondered why our generation remains the same, day in day out, in spite of the fact that this generation has heard more preaching than all the generations of the past put together? Most of our present-day preaching goes unheeded because the vessels preaching are dirty. No decent person will accept food, no matter how good it is, served on a dirty plate. Dirty vessels cannot impact lives, nor can dirty vessels influence and transform lives for the better. Preachers and church workers living in all forms of lust may gather, but not unto Christ. These people may look decent and bask with health, but they are crippled, lame, blind, hungry and naked. And when the head is sick, the body is sick, too.

If preachers do not give people the real life and the truth, the devil will give them the counterfeit, the lies like Islam. If we do not take care of people by fixing ourselves, the devil will get them fixed in all kinds of mysticisms. If we don't get the young people, cults will catch them. We must stop looking complicated, unreachable and unavailable. How many dear souls have perished because a preacher was too busy, unavailable and unreachable for them to get to him to find the solution for their lives? Stop making the faith mysterious and complicated with sophisticated, high-sounding, unattainable messages. The Gospel is simple — *"...Believe in the Lord Jesus Christ...and you will be saved...and your household as well"* (Acts 16:31). The Word will change and transform lives drastically. It will damage the old life — what it was — and make it what God wants it to be.

If we preachers will get right, our people will get right. Like sheep, like shepherd. Like Father, like son. Do not expect your sheep to be what you are not. There is a transfer of spirits from the head to his followers. What you are in your secret place and who you are in your closet are what will affect the people. If it's wrong, they will experience a dark atmosphere of oppression and uncertainties. This makes them vulnerable to all forms of doctrines of devils and all sorts of lying mysticisms.

Many of our well-to-do preachers today would resign from preaching if the possibilities of making money were to be removed from the ministry. We are preaching for bread's sake. The singular, old-fashioned reason for preaching was to spread the Gospel of the Kingdom and to make Jesus known. So old-fashioned preaching that points out sin and prescribes solutions has become history in too many churches. The hard preaching against sin is now called judgmental preaching. Paul revived his generation with this kind of preaching. If we intend to get the same results as Paul, revive our generation and keep the banner of the Gospel of the Kingdom flying, then we must follow his example as he followed Christ.

I believe and sincerely hope it will be in my lifetime that black men who marry white women and vis-a-vis, will find their children accepted without prejudice in both the black and the white communities. I am looking for the time when the black man can walk freely in a white community without stirring up wrong feelings. I am looking for the time when all people in Christ will respect one another, though they may be of diverse colors. When this happens, there will be no stopping the Church. Many religions will fold, because their members will want to belong to a community which is committed to helping one another, regardless of color, creed, race, or position.

When Elijah Mohammed founded Islam in America, he was forced to do so as a reaction against the injustices, prejudices, differences and color preferential treatment he saw in the communities, especially in the church. So if we remove all these cankerworms, the foundation upon which all these other faiths made their converts from among the church, will crumble with a loud crash and the banner of the cross will be raised in their place. We must understand that though Elijah Mohammed claimed Allah told him Islam would save the blacks from oppression and that Islam originated from the blacks, Allah threw down the Koran in America for the blacks, he was making all these false claims out of reactionary emotion and not out of genuine contact with any Allah.

Islam is not a religion of blacks. It originated from the Arabs. There are blue-eyed Moslems all over the world in Europe, Asia and elsewhere. Neither is Islam indigenous to the United States of America. The headquarters of all Islamic faiths is in Mecca. No one can change that. If the Church will clean up its act, all such baseless beliefs will crash with one blow!

14

Biblical Abuse, Misinterpretation and Blasphemy by Islamic Scholars

H. M. Baagil, in his book, *Christian Muslim Dialogue*, quoted extensively from the Bible to prove that Mohammed and Islam were clearly talked about in the Bible, but Christians are too blind to see it. I wonder then, if Dr. H. M. Baagil and his fellow Muslims believe that the Bible has been abrogated due to its corruption by Christians, why should it form any authentic basis for which to prove the authenticity of Islam and its messenger? If they believe the Bible to still be relevant, why not believe its total message? Why pick out only portions of it that you want? If one part is corrupted, then how are we sure that the verses they are picking have not been corrupted too?

Baagil also tried unsuccessfully to prove that Abraham was the first Moslem and that Isaac and Jacob were Moslems. These people were made Moslems by Dr. Baagil because they submitted to "Allah." Abraham spoke Hebrew and never called God "Allah" but Eloha or Elohim, meaning the Creator. Allah has no original meaning, even in Arabic. Arabs used to call the Almighty God Al-Ilah and not Allah. The word *Allah* was fashioned later for an idol god who was seen as the representative of Al-Ilah. So Moslems really are not serving the Almighty God (Al-Ilah), but the fetish called "Allah," who has been hidden at the dome of

167

the rock where people go to bow down to him during every pilgrimage.

While it is true that Abraham is the root of the Arabs through Ishmael, it is not true that Abraham worshipped Allah, as Allah was not in existence then. Ishmael was the illegitimate child, the child of error and mistake. Isaac was the son of promise, and all Israelites are his direct descendants. God promised to bless Ishmael, but only with a nation. However, he was not to be a religious man or a peaceful person. His descendants were covered with the spirit that was to follow him:

> "And the angel of the Lord said unto her, Behold, thou art with child, and shalt bear a son, and shalt call his name Ishmael; because the Lord hath heard thy affliction. And he will be a wild man; his hand will be against every man, and every man's hand against him; and he shall dwell in the presence of all his brethren" (Genesis 16:11-12 KJV).

Note, Abraham did not choose a name for the child, but God named him. God said Ishmael would be a man of struggles, a wild man. *Wild* suggests a troublesome man, a man of war. He would not know peace, neither would he be the founder of a peaceful religion. Instead, he would be reckless, unsound, untamed, impracticable, especially in finance, commerce and social life. *Wild* also means unofficial, uncultivated, irresponsible, rash, reckless, deranged, frenzied, riotous, easily startled, hard to get near to on a friendly basis, unmanageable, uncivilized, savage, desolate, wasteful, unsettled, violent, boisterous, uncontrolled, stormy, obscenely passionate, distracted, mad, out of control, uproarious, immoral, lewd, promiscuous and wasteful. No wonder the Arabs have all kind of troubles and woes. All of these qualities fit exactly into the lifestyle of Ishmael and all Ishmaelites (Arabs). Ask me why the Middle East is as problematic as it is today, and I will show you the reason. The religion that the descendants of Ishmael produced cannot but be wild and untamed. Anyone who embraces such a religion, embraces or subscribes to the wild spirit of Ishmael. Like father, like son; like prophet, like disciples.

The blessing of Abraham did not pass to Ishmael but to Isaac. Though Abraham was not an Israelite, all Israelites are recipients of God's blessings through Abraham. The term *Jew* does not refer to all Hebrews, but to people of the tribe of Judah. However, it came to be used for all Hebrews as a critical nickname, just as followers of Christ are called Christians.

Ablution

The Islamic practice of washing of face, arms, feet and moistening of the hair and falling down on their faces, knocking their foreheads on the ground, is seen as an act of submission. Nowhere in the Koran or in the Bible does God demand that at every worship, this must be done. There were times when God demanded that Moses take off his shoes because the ground on which he was standing was holy ground. It was not a permanent requirement. At times in Moses' relationship with God and the children of Israel, they were commanded to remove their shoes. They never had to wash their faces or knock their heads on the ground. In the New Testament of the Bible, all these religious observances were made obsolete by the Gospel of grace.

God is not interested in the physical posture in worship, but rather in the attitude of a man's heart. Many people cover their sin with religious, legalistic observances. However, Christians do pray with bended knees, bowed heads in an attitude of humility. But these attributes do not concern God as much as the attitude of one's heart and his actions.

God Is Angry With Those Who Bow in Worship to the East

Bowing down to the east at the direction of the sun was prophesied against by Ezekiel. This is what the Moslems do. God prophesied against this style of worship hundreds of years before the religion of Islam came to being. Moslems all over the world pray, bowing to the east. Here is God's injunction:

> *"And He brought me to the inner court of the Lord's house; and behold, at the door of the temple of the Lord, between the porch and the bronze altar, were about twenty-five men with their backs to the temple of the Lord and their faces toward the east, and they were bowing themselves toward the east and worshiping the sun...Therefore I will deal in wrath; My eye will not spare, nor will I have pity; and though they cry in My ears with a loud voice, yet will I not hear them"* (Ezekiel 8:16,18).

Baagil quotes Acts 21:26 which talks about the purification Paul did as an ablution. But the purification of the Hebrew had nothing to do with the washing of face, knees, legs, hands and hair. Their purification was observed for a total period of about seven days. It was purification and not ablution. Neither did Paul keep doing this every time he went to the temple for prayer. So let no one deceive you that Abraham or Jacob or Isaac ever kept removing their shoes or took a certain posture to pray.

Abraham never performed any pilgrimage, neither did any of the prophets in the Old Testament. The Bethel of Palestine is not the Ka'bah. The Ka'bah is in Mecca, but the Padan-aran of Genesis 28:18-19 is in Bethel, which is presently located in Israel. Baagil erred when he said in his book that the Bethel of Jacob was at Ka'bah of Mecca. Jacob never went to Mecca. Neither did any of the prophets of the Bible. Ka'bah holds no religious value to God.

Isaiah 21:7

Baagil quotes Isaiah 21:7 to mean that Jesus came on donkeys, but Mohammed was to come on the camels which were to come after the donkeys.

> *"When he sees chariots with teams of horses, riders on donkeys or riders on camels, let him be alert, fully alert"* (Isaiah 21:7 NIV).

This scripture has nothing to do with Christ or Mohammed. It was a prophecy against Egypt and Cush, telling them to prepare because an army coming on horses, donkeys, or camels would invade the land. Jesus did not ride on donkeys but on a mule colt. And if this scripture means Jesus was going to come riding on donkeys and then Mohammed would come riding on camels, who was it then who was to come before Christ on the horses as suggested by the verse? It is good to note that Jesus never rode on a donkey before or after He rode the colt on the triumphant entry into Jerusalem. So again, Baagil shows his complete ignorance and lack of scholarly intelligence by trying to force this verse to say what he wants. Mohammed was never prophesied in the Bible, as Baagil claims through this verse.

Luke 1:2-3

"Even as they delivered them unto us, which from the beginning were eyewitnesses, and ministers of the word; It seemed good to me also, having had perfect understanding of all things from the very first, to write unto thee in order, most excellent Theophilus" (Luke 1:2-3 KJV).

Baagil uses this as evidence against the inspiration of the Bible. Since Luke said it was an eyewitness account, Baagil wonders how it could then be inspired by God. If this condemns the validity of inspiration of the Bible, then the Koran itself holds no hope of credibility. Because Mohammed was an illiterate, he could not write what the so-called angel told him. Could it be that his illiteracy masked or impaired the accuracy of his reception and understanding of the messages he received? How could we then believe those who scribbled the Koran from Mohammed's followers so many years after he died? How are we sure that the illiteracy of Mohammed did not reduce his ability to deliver whatever message he heard from the so-called angel?

In the normal world judicial system, the account of three eyewitnesses is good enough to condemn a man. The Bible says, "At the mouth of two or three witnesses shall a judgment be confirmed." (See 2 Corinthians 13:1.) The witnesses who confirmed the story and inspiration of the Holy Spirit were more than two or three, and these witnesses wrote their inspirations from different geographical areas and historical times. The inspiration of the Bible is not seen in the same light as Mohammed got his from an angel. Biblical inspiration means holy men were moved by the Holy Spirit to lead the people into all truth. Most of the Scriptures were written by the men themselves, not by a secondary scribe. Except for the book of Luke and Acts, written by Doctor Luke who was a disciple of one of the apostles, all other New Testament records were made by firsthand apostles or witnesses. They did not have to be understood by scribes who had the disadvantage of writing what they did not have the foggiest idea about. If the inspiration of the Bible could be condemned for its report by eyewitnesses, then the Koran should be dumped as original trash or garbage, since the original witness himself, Mohammed, wrote nothing. Third-hand, fourth-hand, or fifth-hand wrote their reports as they believed Mohammed received them from the so-called angel.

Holiness of the Bible

Baagil compares and contrasts scriptures like 2 Samuel 8:4 with 1 Chronicles 18:4 to condemn the holiness of the Bible, because it has such so-called errors of figures.

> *"And David took from him a thousand chariots, and* **seven hundred** *horsemen, and twenty thousand footmen..."*
> (2 Samuel 8:4 KJV).

> *"And David took from him a thousand chariots, and* **seven thousand** *horsemen, and twenty thousand footmen..."*
> (1 Chronicles 18:4 KJV).

Disparity in figures, such as these, are not errors of inspiration. They do not affect the substance of the message of the Bible. The holiness of the Bible is based on the fact that it tells the truth about its chief characters. It does not cover them up where they failed. When David sinned and took Uriah's wife, the Bible does not excuse him. God dealt severely with him. This is so unlike the Koran where Mohammed covers up his evils with a special revelation or injunction from the so-called angel. The Bible does not lie about its facts. This is what makes it holy. The Bible does not cover up the temptations of Jesus. But the Koran never believes that Mohammed, though an ordinary man, ever was tempted nor did he ever fail or sin. I find that really dubious and misleading.

Baagil condemns David for committing adultery and disputes the fact that such a man could be in the lineage of Christ. I can understand and sympathize with Baagil, because in Islam, you never experience pardon while here on earth. Yet the Bible proclaims pardon to its subjects who have failed. This is what makes the Bible holy. It never lies about anyone or any situation. When God forgives a man, He forgets that the person ever sinned.

> *"...Their sins and lawless acts I will remember no more"*
> (Hebrews 10:17 NIV).

This promise was made to the children of Israel, including David.

> *"As far as the east is from the west, so far has he removed our transgressions from us"* (Psalm 103:12 NIV).

This is from David himself. God removed his sins from him, so it was not too much that God would allow Christ to come through his lineage.

Luke 12:51-53

Baagil suggests in his book (page 37, paragraph 2) that Jesus did not come to bring peace. He says Jeremiah gave peace as a criterion of the prophet.

> *"The prophet which prophesieth of peace, when the word of the prophet shall come to pass, then shall the prophet be known, that the Lord hath truly sent him"* (Jeremiah 28:9 KJV).

The word *Islam* also signifies tranquillity, peace — peace between the Creator and His creatures. This prophecy of Jeremiah cannot be applied to Jesus, as He stated that He didn't come for peace on earth.

> *"Do not think that I have come to bring peace upon the earth; I have not come to bring peace, but a sword. For I have come to part asunder a man from his father, and a*

daughter from her mother, and a newly married wife from her mother-in-law" (Matthew 10:34,35).

Until Shiloh Come

"Until Shiloh come" was a message of Jacob to his children before he died:

> *"And Jacob called unto his sons, and said, Gather yourselves together, that I may tell you that which shall befall you in the last days"* (Genesis 49:1 KJV).

Genesis 49:10 KJV says:

> *"The sceptre shall not depart from Judah, nor a lawgiver from between his feet, until Shiloh come; and unto him shall the gathering of the people be."*

Shiloh is also the name of a town, but its real meaning is peace, tranquillity, rest; i.e., Islam. It could never refer to town. If it referred to a person, it could be a corruption of Shaluah (Elohim); i.e., messenger (of Allah).

So the Israelite prophethood in the lineage of Isaac would stop as soon as Shiloh comes. This corresponds with Surah 2:133: "Were you witnesses when death came to Jacob, when he said to his sons, 'What will you worship after me?' They said, 'We shall worship your God (Allah), the God of your fathers Abraham, Ishmael and Isaac, One God and to Him we surrender (in Islam).'"

The shift of prophethood to another nation was threatened in Jeremiah 31:36 KJV:

> *"If those ordinances depart from before me, saith the Lord, then the seed of Israel also shall cease from being a nation before me for ever."*

Also hinted by Jesus in Matthew 21:43 KJV:

> *"Therefore say I unto you, The kingdom of God shall be taken from you, and given to a nation bringing forth the fruits thereof."*

Baagil completely misunderstands and misinterprets the Bible, as all other Moslems, because he is not approaching it in the spirit of the Bible, but with a spirit of condemnation and contradiction.

At the birth of Christ, the angels said:

> *"Glory to God in the highest, and on earth peace, good will toward men"* (Luke 2:14 KJV).

The chief reason why Jesus came was to bring and make peace between God and man.

Jesus believed in and preached peace. When He sent His disciples out, He told them to first seek for the son of peace and to greet the people with peace.

> *"And into whatsoever house ye enter, first say, Peace be to this house"* (Luke 10:5 KJV).

He came to give peace:

> *"Peace I leave with you, my peace I give unto you..."* (John 14:27 KJV).

> *"These things I have spoken unto you, that in me ye might have peace. In the world ye shall have tribulation: but be of good cheer; I have overcome the world"* (John 16:33 KJV).

This peace was not the peace of Islam but the peace of God which comes from being sure that you are already saved from hell and are heading to heaven, and that your name is written in the book of life.

Baagil abuses and misinterprets Luke 12:51-53 to mean Jesus came to bring enmity and not peace, so He does not qualify to be a prophet. The true Biblical meaning of these verses was to correct the views of the disciples who thought that Christ had come to give them external peace politically with their colonizers, but instead, He came to give them internal peace of heart. So the disciples were to brace up to bear the hardships and difficulties.

The effect of preaching the Gospel will be external division. If a member of a Moslem family repents and returns to Christ, the rest of the members of his family will persecute him. In this way, the Gospel has not brought him peace externally with his Moslem parents and brothers. In the same way, if a member of an unbelieving family repents, the rest will surely hate him, but the person who repented will experience great peace internally.

Christ brings perfect peace into the lives and homes of those who fully receive Him. Everyone who has experienced the born again touch is always put in proper order and shape. The design of the Gospel is to unite the children of men to one another, to knit them together in holy love, and if all the world receives it, the effect of it will be peace. But there are multitudes who will not only reject it, but oppose it and have their corruptions exasperated by it. They become enraged at those who do receive it, like the Moslem antagonist. In this way, it proves to be an occasion for necessary division.

Dr. Baagil also quotes Genesis 49:10 KJV:

> "The sceptre shall not depart from Judah, nor a lawgiver from between his feet, until Shiloh come; and unto him shall the gathering of the people be."

He goes on to say that Shiloh is talking of Shaluah (Elohim); i.e., messenger of Allah. This is another intentional move to misrepresent, misinterpret, abuse and force the Bible to say what it does not say. Mohammed was born an Ishmaelite, the son of a bondwoman. How could he become Shiloh, a descendant of Judah? God never threatened to shift the sceptre from Judah. The sceptre was to be in Judah forever. The verse says, "This sceptre shall not depart...." Jesus was born under the tribe of Judah. When He went about preaching, people in great crowds followed Him. At His death, great crowds were present. This scripture was speaking of Christ. Baagil says God shifted the Shiloh to Mohammed because of Jeremiah 31:36. That verse does not speak of Judah or Shiloh but of Israel. That scripture did not come to pass because Israel still existed as a people. At the time of Christ, Israel still existed as a nation, so this verse, even if God wiped out the nation of Israel today, Shiloh had already come 2,000 years ago.

Baca Is Not Mecca

Dr. Baagil says:

"The Holy Kabah built by Abraham and his son Ishmael is in Mecca. This name Mecca (Makkah) has been mentioned one time in the Holy Qur'an in Surah 48:24. Another name for Mecca is Bakka, depending on the dialect of the tribe. This also has been mentioned one time, in Surah 3:96: "Verily, the first House [of worship] appointed for mankind was that in Bakka [Mecca], full of blessing, and guidance for all people." Amazing enough, this word *Bakka* was mentioned by Prophet David [PBUH] in his Psalm 84:6 KJV: *"Who passing through the valley of Baca make it a well; the rain also filleth the pools."* The *well* here is the well-known well of Zamzam, still present now, close to the Kabah."

Abraham never enjoined Ishmael to build Ka'bah in Mecca. Abraham never journeyed through Saudi Arabia according to the Biblical or Koranic account. In fact, after Ishmael and his mother ran out of the house, Abraham never set his eyes on the lad again until he died.

"...And when Sarai dealt hardly with her, she fled from her face" (Genesis 16:6 KJV).

The valley of Baca referred to in Psalm 84:6 was a pitted, marshy and miry valley through which a road was constructed in the land of Israel leading to Jerusalem. Baca is in Israel and not in Mecca. Baca does not mean Makkah or Mecca or Bakka, regardless of the dialect you use. Makka or Bakka or Mecca is hundreds of miles away from Baca. Psalm 84:6 does not say there is a well of ZamZam in the valley of Baca, but it says those who pass through it, instead of weeping because of the difficulty experienced in passing it, have made a well out of the situation. This is not a literal well, but it is another way of saying, "They have turned its disadvantage to advantage." In actuality, the valley of Baca means the weeping valley, because of the drainages constructed in the valley to drain water away from the road constructed in the marshy land.

The Bible never mentioned Mecca, either in the New or Old Testament. Baagil's abusive misinterpretations of the Bible can be clearly seen, even by babies in Christ, as being intentional to mislead and misguide honest seekers of God and His salvation from sins through Christ.

Baagil also gives an extensive quoting of Isaiah 60:11 KJV where it says:

> "Therefore thy gates shall be open continually; they shall not be shut day nor night; that men may bring unto thee the forces of the Gentiles, and that their kings may be brought."

He then goes on to misrepresent this verse by saying, "It is a fact that the mosque surrounding the holy Ka'bah in Mecca has remained open day and night since it was cleansed by prophet Mohammed from the idols 1,400 years ago. Rulers as well as subjects came for pilgrimage."

In verse 10, the Bible says God smote the walls of this city, referred to in verse 11, in His wrath. But this wall shall be rebuilt and the gates put in place. Then shall visitors come to see. This city is Jerusalem. It has a wall around it with twelve gates. Though Jerusalem is receiving all kinds of pilgrims from all over the world today, the fulfillment of this scripture, Isaiah 60:1-4, shall come to pass during the millennial reign of Christ. In verse 3, Isaiah talks of Gentiles. This word is not an Arabic word. It is a Hebrew expression for those who are not Hebrews by birth. So Arabs are also Gentiles. They are going to be part of the host that must serve Christ at Jerusalem during the millennium or be expunged.

It is only to Israel, therefore, that all Gentiles will gather. In no way do these verses talk of the pilgrimage to Mecca. Can we feel safe to say that these verses were referring to Chicago, New York and Hawaii because their airports are never closed day and night because of the influx of tourists? The fact that pilgrims from all over the world go to Mecca does not automatically mean that Isaiah was speaking of Mecca, since Isaiah specifically mentioned that Gentiles will be the ones traveling to this city. A Gentile city like Mecca, which never had any prophetic or religious importance, could not be spoken of so elaborately like that.

On page 39 of his book, Baagil interprets verses in Isaiah, not having the foggiest idea what they are about, trying to force the verses to mean what he wants them to say. In all his assumptions, he used "probably." *Probably* is wishful thinking, but it is surely not his probabilities. Mohammed may have ridden on camels, but Baagil being from Kuwait, should have known that through the land of Israel, camels were not an uncommon sight. Can we say all the verses in the Bible that talked of camels from the land of Midian, Persia, Medes and Egypt were referring to Mohammed? This would be like saying that because Japan makes so many cars for export that everyone driving a Japanese car is a Japanese.

Baagil continues his blunder by quoting Deuteronomy 18:18 KJV:

> *"I will raise them up a Prophet from among their brethren, like unto thee* [Moses], *and will put my words in his mouth...."*

He goes on to say this prophet referred to prophet Mohammed, that God would raise this prophet from the "brethren" of Israelites and not from among the Israelites, so Jesus was excluded.

Could Baagil be joking? Or, does he really mean he does not understand who a brother is? Or, is he intentionally twisting the Bible? When you say, "My brethren," you simply mean, "My people, my own flesh and blood brother." So when God said, "From *among* their brethren," He meant from among their brothers. That means your own flesh and blood, meaning Christ.

Mohammed was not like Moses in any spiritual way. When God said the prophet would be like Moses, he was not talking of his birth, family life, death, career, forced immigration, encounter with enemies or the reception and writing down of revelation, the nature of teachings, or the acceptability of his leadership by his people. But the prophet, like Moses, was going to be by birth. He would live among them and be sent to them like Moses was. His death would also be on the mountain, like Moses. As Moses was a lawgiver to Israel and a deliverer from Egypt, so was Christ. He not only teaches, but rules, saves and delivers from sin and hell. Moses founded a new dispensation by *signs* and *wonders* and mighty *deeds*, and so did Christ. Moses was faithful, and so was Christ. By signs and wonders and mighty deeds alone, Mohammed stands a million miles away from being compared with Moses. Mohammed did no signs or wonders or mighty deeds.

The verse also says he who does not listen to this prophet shall be bearing his own blood. No wonder in John 3:18,36 the Bible says:

> *"He who believes in Him* [Christ] *[who clings to, trusts in, relies on Him] is not judged [he who trusts in Him never comes up for judgment; for him there is no rejection, no condemnation — he incurs no damnation]; but he who does not believe (cleave to, rely on, trust in Him) is judged already [he has already been convicted and has already received his sentence] because he has not believed in and trusted in the name of the only begotten Son of God. [He is condemned for refusing to let his trust rest in Christ's name.]*
>
> *"And he who believes in (has faith in, clings to, relies on) the Son has (now possesses) eternal life. But **whoever disobeys** (is unbelieving toward, refuses to trust in, disregards, is not subject to) the Son will never see (experience) life, but [instead] the wrath of God abides on him. [God's displeasure remains on him; His indignation hangs over him continually.]"*

Deuteronomy 18:18 said God will put His words into the mouth of this prophet. Jesus said in John 7:16:

> *"...My teaching is not My own, but His Who sent Me."*

Whatever messages God had to send to the world, He put in the lips of Jesus to speak as a "prophet." Mohammed never foretold a thing after the manner of a prophet. The verse did not say whoever refuses the religion of the prophet will be punished, but *whoever does not accept the teachings of such a prophet will be damned.* The focus is on the prophet, not on religion. Christianity is based on the convert's acceptance of Christ and His claims of sonship or oneness with the Father.

Christianity Is for Gentiles

Jesus spoke to the Canaanite woman who brought her daughter to Him for healing:

> *"Let the children **first** be filled: for it is not meet to take the children's bread, and to cast it unto the dogs"* (Mark 7:27 KJV).

Baagil connects this verse with Matthew 10:5-6 and 15:24 where Jesus said He was sent only to the lost sheep of the house of Israel. He then goes on to show his total ignorance about Christian doctrines by claiming that Christianity was meant only for Israel as is proved in Mark 7:26. But when the Israelites turned their back on the Gospel, the Gentiles who were supposed to have had a secondary place in hearing the Gospel, became the first. So the Gospel broke the dividing line between Jews and Gentiles, Greeks and Samaritans. In fact, the Gospel broke the dividing line of tribe, creed, nationality, or race.

Black, white, brown, red and yellow all qualify to become Christians. Jesus died for all. No wonder He sent Paul to the Gentiles:

> *"But the Lord said unto him, Go thy way: for he is a chosen vessel unto me, **to bear my name before the Gentiles**, and kings, and the children of Israel"* (Acts 9:15 KJV).

> *"Is he the God of the Jews only? is he not also of the Gentiles? Yes, of the Gentiles also: Seeing it is one God, which shall justify the circumcision by faith, and uncircumcision through faith"* (Romans 3:29,30 KJV).

When Jesus referred to the Canaanite lady as a dog, He simply was trying to stand by the Jewish frame of mind that all those outside the twelve tribes of Israel were dogs. Today, all those who are outside the Kingdom of God are also called dogs. But dogs can be converted if they repent.

Baagil moves his misguided blunders to Isaiah 42. He picks the word *messenger* in verses 1 and 19 to mean Mohammed, since he was the only one ever called "Abduha wa Rasuluhul Mustapha"; i.e., his slave servant and his elected messenger. Where in the Bible or even in the Qur'an was Mohammed filled with the Holy Spirit as these verses suggest? Without the evidence of the Spirit, these verses could be claimed by any prophet — Shinto, Buddha, Krishna, Moon, etc. But the dividing line is the seal and signature of God's approval by a public show of the filling of the Spirit. This happened only to Christ as is proven in Matthew 3:16-17 and Luke 9:35.

> *"And Jesus, when he was baptized, went up straightway out of the water: and, lo, the heavens were opened unto him, and he saw the Spirit of God descending like a dove, and lighting upon him: And lo a voice from heaven, saying, This is my beloved Son, in whom I am well pleased"* (Matthew 3:16-17 KJV).

Now compare this with Isaiah 42:1 KJV:

> *"Behold my servant, whom I uphold; mine elect, in whom my soul delighteth [or I am well pleased]; I have put my spirit upon him...."*

To prove to you that Isaiah 42 was talking about Christ, read verse 7.

> *"To open the blind eyes...."*

Blind eyes here means physically and not just darkness from which people need to turn. Mohammed never opened any blind eyes, but Jesus opened the eyes of blind men. This scripture portrays qualities that Mohammed, in his lifetime, never fulfilled.

Mohammed raised his voice and hand against his enemies and even friends. In comparison, though Jesus was disappointed over His rejection by the Israelites, He mourned for their ignorance.

Baagil said Mohammed was referred to as one of the Lord's in Psalm 110:1 KJV:

"The Lord said unto my Lord...."

Two Lords are mentioned here. Baagil agrees in the authority and authenticity of both Lords, only to him one must be Mohammed and the other Christ. All along, Baagil said Mohammed was only a slave of God and he [Mohammed] never claimed to be equal with God. In the meantime, Christ, Who lived 600 years before him, said, *"I and the Father are one."* So in Psalm 110:1, David meant that the Lord God said to David's Lord, Who is Christ. So the two "Lords" here are the *Lord God Jehovah* and the *Lord Jesus Christ*, not Mohammed. Mohammed was a slave. His usual birth from a sinful father and mother disqualifies him from being Lord.

Baagil also says that John the Baptist talked of the One coming Who will baptize with the Holy Ghost and fire (Matthew 3:11). He asks if this was not Mohammed that John spoke of. My answer is an emphatic no. It was not Mohammed who John was speaking of, for Mohammed never baptized with the Holy Ghost and fire. But Jesus baptized with the Holy Ghost and fire. (See Acts 2:1-19.)

Baagil finally quotes from Isaiah 29:12 KJV to prove that Mohammed was predicted in the Bible.

"And the book is delivered to him that is not learned, saying, Read this, I pray thee: and he saith, I am not learned."

In the Qur'an, we are not told that the angel handed Mohammed a book, only that he was asked to recite. Now *to recite* is different from reading. It means, "Repeat after me." So the so-called angel asked Mohammed to repeat and not to read, as the angel was supposed to be speaking to Mohammed with his voice. At that time, no Quran had been written, so he could not have been asked to read from it!

In this passage, God asked Isaiah to give the book to the community to read, but because it was written prophetically, they could not understand what it meant. They were not illiterates as Mohammed, but they were not taught in the school of the prophets to understand prophecies and interpret them. If Moslems want this verse to refer to Mohammed, they must be ready to take the following scriptural damnation of verses 13-14. This also applies to Mohammed and to Moslems in general. It says:

> "Wherefore the Lord said, Forasmuch as this people draw near me with their mouth, and with their lips do honour me, but have removed their heart far from me, and their fear toward me is taught by the precept of men: Therefore...their wise men shall perish, and the understanding of their prudent men shall be hid."

The other tongue of Isaiah 28:10-11 Baagil says is not Hebrew or Aramaic but Arabic. Why should the tongue be Arabic? It could as well be Chinese, Japanese, Korean, or Hausa. The tongue referred to here is the same with the one referred to in Jude 20, 1 Corinthians 13:1 and 1 Corinthians 14:2. Isaiah was referring to the unknown tongues that people were to receive from Christ after He baptizes them with the Holy Ghost and fire. Arabic is not called a tongue; it is a language. It is understood by men, and it is the tongue of men. But Isaiah says the tongue he is referring to will not be understood by men because it will be strange.

Finally, people like Baagil love to twist Bible verses so as to confuse unlearned church people and lead them blindfolded into Islam.

The lives of people who twist Scripture shall not last long or end well. This not only applies to Moslems who twist the Bible to suit their purposes, but also to Christian liberal theologians who abuse the Bible.

Let's all heed the warning of Peter in 2 Peter 3:16-17:

> *"...There are some things in those [epistles of Paul] that are difficult to understand, which the **ignorant** and **unstable twist and misconstrue to their own utter destruction**, just as [they **distort** and **misinterpret**] the rest of the Scriptures.*
>
> *"Let me warn you therefore, beloved, that knowing these things beborehand, **you should be on your guard, lest you be carried away by the error of lawless and wicked [persons and] fall from your own [present] firm condition** [your own steadfastness of mind]."*

Hear the warnings of John in the book of Revelation, chapter 22, verses 18-19, KJV:

> *"...If any man shall add unto these things, God shall add unto him the plagues that are written in this book: And if any man shall take away from the words of the book of this prophecy, God shall take away his part out of the book of life...."*

Finally, if Dr. H. M. Baagil and all his Moslem friends believe so much in the authority of the Bible as to make Mohammed and Islam a credible way of life, then they should also believe the rest of the Bible. John 3:5 KJV says:

> *"...Except a man be born of water and of the Spirit, he cannot enter into the kingdom of God."*

I sincerely pray that they believe this and are born again before the end comes for them. Christians need to prepare and move into the Islamic hinterland and harvest Moslems for the Kingdom of God.

15
The Truth

Jesus is the only remedy for man's damnation. This is not a matter of politics. I am Mada by tribe. He was an Israelite by geographical location. I am black. He was red. The only thing that matters most to me that was in Him was the Spirit of Christ, not of the carpenter who was of Israeli nationality.

The devil tried to bring scandal on Mary before His birth, but nothing can stand against the truth.

Herod attempted assassination of the King of glory in order to stifle the truth about the long awaited fulfillment of prophecies; but shame on the devil, for nothing can stand against the truth.

The Bible, and even the Quran, testify that Jesus went about doing good, healing them who were oppressed of the devil, because of the Spirit of God upon Him. But how could the devil stir up rumors that Jesus was casting out demons by the spirit of Beelzebub? Nothing can withstand the truth.

Some were smart enough to think of implicating Jesus for treason, but nothing can be done against the truth.

The tree that He created was converted into a cross on which He was crucified, giving Him the status of a criminal. But nothing lasting can be done against the truth.

Jesus Christ was resurrected from the dead on the third day in fulfillment of prophecy. Government paid so much to keep the Good News of eternal truth from the masses, but they failed ultimately because nothing can be done against the truth.

Even though the truth has an inherent potential of surviving infinity, the devil still never gives up on confusing the world: To give men wood instead of pure gold and chaff for wheat. The Roman religious leaders desired to keep the Word of life from the people's reach, shifting the attention of men from the Savior to an innocent Mary, but nothing can be done against the truth. Jesus is still the only mediator between God and man. We have been given a name, and there is none other name given among men whereby we can be saved. In the name of Jesus Christ, *all* men have a direct access into the presence of the Father.

Mohammed was possessed by the spirit of the antichrist, who possessed the Roman Catholics to be wicked to Martin Luther and then to Christians. Many Christians were mercilessly injured, thrown to lions and some burned alive because the Roman Catholics wanted to sit on the truth and keep the whole world in religious darkness, but it was just a matter of time, and the truth prevailed! Praise God.

The Church was added to the Israelites, the Protestants were added to the Catholics, the Pentecostals to the Protestants, the Charismatics to the Pentecostals, the Word of Life to the Charismatics — and this will continue until Jesus comes, because nothing can be done against the truth.

There are many indications in the Quran to prove that Jesus died. These include Sura 3:54-56 and 19:33. But these mean nothing to the Moslems, because they are bent on carrying on faithfully the heretic teachings of their misguided leader. However, nothing can be done against the truth.

A group of film actors some years back came up with a fantasy production, portraying Jesus Christ as a homosexual. The American government wouldn't have been able to stop those creative personalities in their apostatic adventure. And in spite of captivating fallacies, the whole world still trembles at the mention of the name of Jesus. Of course, the spirit of the antichrist could not stop the world from recognizing the distinction between Jesus, the true Messiah, and a mere cinema character. The film has come and gone. It died a natural death, because nothing can prevail against the truth.

Uthman Dan Fodio entered Ilorin with his own Islamic massacre, slaughtering Christians and other non-Muslims in order to install Islam. He couldn't enter into Ogbomoso, because the prevailing demons during the idol worshipping era were too strong for the Islamic god. But when Christianity came with just the Bible, music and a smile to preach the Good News, Ogbomoso was captured without firing one bullet or mortar, and it became the Jerusalem of the Nigerian Baptist Church until this day. Praise God! People who repented gave up their Idols willingly and carvings worth millions of dollars were burned.

The Bible says we are being killed and counted as sheep for the slaughter every day, yet we are more than conquerors through Him Who loves us (Romans 8:36-37). Why? Because nothing can be done against the truth.

I could go on and on to stress the fact that the truth always prevails, even if it takes centuries of concealing the truth. Like the dawning of the day, truth will prevail at last, after the long night hours of shadow, darkness and mystery, ignorance, confusion and falsehood.

In fact, I fail to see the reason why a special award was given for the head of Salman Rushdie, the author of Satanic Verses, because truth always prevails.

Many religions have tried to mutilate Scripture to justify carnal, selfish, inconsiderate and inconsistent doctrinal values and political gimmicks: Quoting the Bible out of context, furnishing people with heretic commentaries on certain scriptures to make them say or mean what was not intended. But even with all these expensive and rigorous attempts, truth still stands for itself and can never be confused with falsehood, no matter how glittering it looks.

However, there is always room for "itching ears," because it has been prophesied 2,000 years ago whereby children of disobedience conceal carnal hearts' desires and selectively filter out of the Bible for the purpose of argument, competition and grandfather contentions.

Some Islamic jihadists are beginning to parade themselves around Africa, Europe and America these days. They are only servants, ordinary slaves of Allah, but the Son is always the Son of God. He is the Lion of the Church. He will always be a lion, whether in the zoo or in the forest. No matter how the Islamic murderers promise to improve our political stability, the truth still remains — they are children of their father, the devil, who seeks to steal, kill and destroy. But the Son of God, the Lion from the tribe of Judah, came that we might have life and have it more abundantly (John 10:10). No matter what, a lion is still a lion. It shall clean the forest of all other small monkey religions, all the flukes. It's just a matter of time!

Mohammed was asked one day, "Where are you going (after death)?" and he replied that he didn't know. Imagine then, what would be the hope of a blind follower who is being led by another blind man? But Jesus said, *"I am the way, the truth, and the life: no man cometh unto the Father, but by me"* (John 14:6 KJV). No matter how a counterfeit object resembles an original, it is still not the original. Only truth will set man free. For the Bible says, *"And ye shall know the truth, and the truth shall make you free"* (John 8:32 KJV).

An old imam who owned a mosque at Lekki village confessed Christ during one of our team members' missionary trips to Lagos peninsula in 1993. He confessed before his antagonistic wife, "Indeed, you Christians are holier and more godly, that is the truth...." He asked Jesus to save him, and team members prayed for him. His wife tried to stop him from what she called "desecrating" Islam, but reality had dawned on him at an old age. And he could no longer help but identify with the Man Who knows the way to the Father. He identified with the truth at last.

I am saying, with all conviction, that any nation that opens her doors to Islam, is heading towards destruction. When Christianity was the mainstay of Egypt, the country was known as one of the centers of scientific discovery and excellence. Medical science was improved in that nation in those days of Christianity. As soon as Islam took over the nation by force, all the scientific possibilities disappeared, along with Christianity. Go to Egypt now and you will see the filth, the backwardness, the massive spirit of ignorance and poverty everywhere. This is what happens to a nation when it is overrun by Islam. This is also the ruin of all those families who embrace Islam. Strange tendencies of backwardness set in.

This also happened to Ethiopia, Turkey and all the progressive Christian islands of the Bible days. Because they turned their backs on the Gospel, God, so to speak, turned His back on their developmental possibilities.

As Islam loses its grip on Nigeria and other lands, it is moving to America. Unfortunately, Americans have refused to wake up, dust their Bibles off and reactivate their love for Jehovah. It is because of this that America as a nation is losing her premier position in the world to other smaller nations in the areas of commerce and technology. If the nation refuses to wake up, it will discover the truth only too late. The Bible says it is God Who shuts a door, and when He shuts it, no one can open it; and when He opens a door, no one can shut it (Revelation 3:8). If God Almighty cannot be trusted to solve the problem of racial discrimination in America, then the Allah of Farrakhan, Malcom X, Elijah Mohammed and even Mohammed the Ishmaelite Arab, cannot help. It is too big a task for Allah and his trickster ambassadors.

Besides, it wasn't Allah who appealed to scores of American artists to raise funds and support Ethiopia in 1984. It wasn't Allah who broke the backbone of apartheid in South Africa recently. As far as Mohammed's Allah is concerned, if Moslems were not included among those suffering, it was not his business to help them. Only Moslems are fit to live according to his view. It took God and God alone through the Church and other church-related agencies to dismantle apartheid. We must not forget that and turn to a broken cistern for help.

Where was Louis Farrakhan when Mandela served twenty-five years in prison? Where was Malcom X or Elijah Mohammed? Why did none of them come to the rescue when they were needed the most? Why is mallam Louis Farrakhan just surfacing now after the war has been fought, won and concluded? Why is it that he is just now parading himself as a black man? I smell a rat, a trap set for the unsuspecting American youth.

Jesus is the only One Who can eat with sinners, regardless of complexion or race. Allah of the wild Arabs can't bear it. That is why he instructs his adherents to break our necks and kill us, because we are not of the house of Dar-es-Salam, the house of peace. What apartheid is more than that? What discrimination is worse than that?

I adjure you to seek for the truth of God Almighty and you will be free. Silver is not the same as gold, for those who are interested in the truth. I found the truth in 1975, and since then I have been riding on the wings of the excellency of the truth which Mohammed refers to in Sura 3:55. *Nothing can be truer than the truth!*

Just as the Muslims sought to kill me, they did to others when they found the truth. You cannot kill the truth. They can only kill flesh and blood, and the blood of the martyrs becomes a catalyst for more revival of the truth. Besides, anyone who believes in Christ, though he dies, he shall live again. And you cannot kill a dead man. I died 2,000 years ago and I cannot die again. The life I now live is to the truth. Praise God for everyone seeking the truth. There is only one truth, not two truths. Jesus is that single living truth. For everyone in darkness and misery, Jesus Christ is the Light. For everyone confused and perplexed, Jesus is the only way. And for everyone who has been beaten by the storms of life to the point of coma and helplessness, only Jesus is the way. He may not come today with the needed deliverance. He may not come when you think you need Him, but

He always comes through right on time. Jesus says, *"I am the way, the truth, and the life: no man cometh unto the Father, but by me."* Any nation or people who seek after another god, besides the Father God of our Lord Jesus Christ, will sell themselves to a life of permanent misery.

God revealed to me through past events how Britain, Germany, Spain and now America are forsaking the fountain of living waters and choosing to drink from a filthy cistern of materialism, education, sex, occult and now, Islam! Jesus said categorically that any man or angel who comes with another gospel, we are not to follow him.

Glory to God that Russia, at last, is able to identify with the truth after hundreds of years of futile antagonisms. Shall we then, who have held the truth for so long, turn around and go back to our vomit? No wonder Jesus said the first shall be the last, and the last shall be the first (Matthew 19:30). We must be careful not to let this negative prophecy come to pass in our nations and in our lives. It was not given that it must come to pass, but as a warning not to draw back from God. Karl Marx confessed so many things on his deathbed only he had led countless millions of people to hell. Let's forsake evil and embrace righteousness. Let's join the songwriter and sing, "I don't want the devil's money, I can't give my gold for silver...." The devil has nothing to offer. And when he offers a penny, he takes a pound.

Arise, O ye nations of the earth, for the end is near. Let us join hands together to propagate the truth. Enough of complacency. The devil is not relenting at all, because we are at the eleventh hour. He has never given up on mutilating and fighting the truth, sponsoring evil and propagating falsehood. Recently, it was rumored to us that about 666,000,000 pounds Sterling was paid to Louis Farrakhan in fulfillment of their mission to Islamize the world. Does that figure ring a bell? This is the code of the antichrist — 666. Let him who has an ear hear what the Spirit is saying to the Church.

Every American preacher who is allowing Louis Farrakhan into his church under the guise of black "solidarity" had better be wise and know that, though he is black, he is a Moslem and does not see such preachers in his brotherhood as long as they are Christians. They are of the house of war. If religion demands it, he will definitely not hesitate to lift his hand against such. He is only using these people to achieve his political and religious agenda. Remember, elsewhere Islam does not separate between religion and politics. Farrakhan is in this light, and therefore is the Islamic caliph of the United States of America.

Our youths are very impressionable and gullible and do not know how to separate between the man and the religion. So they are quick to embrace Islam because they see that their parents see nothing wrong in the man. He is even given a triumphant entry into the Church and pulpit of our Lord Jesus Christ! We must wake up and realize that Farrakhan is not our dear Martin Luther King, Jr. Farrakhan has a hidden agenda, and he is subtly selling his goods of merchandise because of our lack of discernment. If he has been paid to do his missionary work, he will spare no promises to get where he wants to go. Don't be deceived. He is nowhere near becoming a Christian, regardless how much he quotes the Bible. Remember, I shared with you earlier how Moslems are using the Bible to try to prove the authenticity of their Quran and prophet. It is therefore no big deal for them to quote the Bible, because they believe the Bible but will not submit to its power. Truth may be truth no matter who says it, but dear friend, of what good is one truth in the midst of a million lies? Even the devil tells the truth sometimes or quotes the Word. Do we therefore accept the devil into our churches and our pulpits because he knows and tells some truths?

Remember, when old Satan wanted to slide Christ away, he quoted some scriptures. He even said, *"It is written."* How foolish are we, then, to allow the devil in disguise to come in and cause division in the Church? If the Church is interested in fair treatment of all races, it ought to rise up and undertake her own campaign and not wait for an Islamic caliph to come into the Church and slide the unsuspecting youths — our seed for future generations — into Islam, a hell-bound lifestyle. The eloquence of Louis Farrakhan is charming the youths to believe Islam is synonymous with eloquence, sharp mouth and sweet tongue.

I believe in black solidarity and freedom the world over, but not at the expense of my salvation or that of my children. Religion is a matter of life and death. No compromise should be made that will be misleading to future generations. The Church alone has the solution to the problems of the world. I say the Church, and for me, the Church is not a black and white thing. It is the Body of Christ. It must, therefore, be closely guarded with the eye of keeping the bond of brotherhood as we work hard towards killing those little foxes who seem to be eating up our vines.

Jesus prayed that the Church may be one. May His prayer not be hindered by our attitudes, but rather be enhanced. Let's quit being like children, never coming to the perfection of the truth, but holding onto mere fleeting shadows of human gimmicks from Islamic stooges like Louis Farrakhan. Don't be deceived, for what fellowship has light with darkness?

"And you shall know the truth, and the truth shall make you free!" If you fail to heed my warning and alarm in this writing, you will live to reap the impact of your actions. Should you hear and turn, you will also reap the impact of your actions.

Jesus is the only begotten Son of God. That is the truth.

Jesus is the Word of God. That is the truth.

Jesus is the only way to God. That is the truth.

Jesus was conceived of the Holy Ghost. That is the truth.

Jesus died for the sins of the world. That is the truth.

Jesus was resurrected from the dead. That is the truth.

Jesus is coming back again. That is the truth.

Jesus shall judge the world. That is the truth.

Jesus is the only key to salvation. That is the truth.

Jesus and the Father are one. That is the truth.

The Holy Spirit of God is our Comforter. That is the truth.

And Jesus is the truth. That is the truth.

What, then, do you intend to do with the truth — Jesus Christ — the Lifegiver, the Savior, the Deliverer, the Healer, the Baptizer, the Apostle and High Priest of our faith, the Lord, the King and the only truth?

You can experience the truth right now by simply inviting Him into your heart. Just say this simple prayer with me:

"Lord Jesus, I do agree that I need You. I have sinned against You. I ask You now to forgive my sins. I agree that You died for me on the cross. I believe that You are the Christ, the Son of the Living God. Therefore, I receive You now as my Savior and Lord. Write my name in the Book of Life in heaven. Thank You for receiving me and for coming into my life. Amen."

You have an Adamic nature of sin, and that nature must die. It must be killed and not just understood. It must be radically transformed into the nature of God that rejoices even in the face of the most stringent hatred, dislike and persecution.

Now that you have given your heart to Jesus, you can turn from your failures and sins. Be completely persuaded about the reality of your commitment to God and change your attitude towards the things of God in a positive direction. Six things happen in your life when you receive Christ:

1. Christ has come into you, just as He promised to do (Revelation 3:20).

2. Your sins are forgiven and forgotten by God (Hebrews 10:17; Colossians 1:14).

3. You have become a child of God (John 1:12).

4. You now have eternal life. You don't have to die to be assured of heaven. You can know it right now. That is why Jesus came (1 John 5:11-13).

5. You are now a new creature, a new person (2 Corinthians 5:17).

6. You can now begin to enjoy a full and satisfying life as Christ lives His life in and through you (John 10:10).

You must do eight things to grow in your new-found faith:

1. Know and believe that Christ will never leave you nor forsake you (Hebrews 13:5).

2. You must now begin to eat the Word of God daily. It is the food for your spirit (1 Peter 2:2).

3. You must spend time talking to God just as you would talk to a friend (1 Thessalonians 5:17).

4. Learn to obey Christ in all things at all times (John 14:21).

5. Continue to live by faith, trusting God for your daily provision (Romans 1:17).

6. Even from your disadvantaged position, from your want or lack, be a constant, generous giver (2 Corinthians 9:6-8; Luke 6:38).

7. Witness for Christ daily by your life and words (Matthew 25:14-30).

8. Receive the baptism of the Holy Ghost. You need a powerful Gospel. Don't settle for old women's fables, but go for the power. Ask God to baptize you in the Holy Ghost. The power of God is still alive and active, as it was when Christ walked this earth (Acts 2:17-21).

Right now, start attending a local church that teaches and practices sound Gospel, the whole Gospel. None of it has passed away. The power is still the same as it was 2,000 years ago.

Write to me today for further help.

16
The Challenge

We must face the Islamic challenge, both within our nations and in the external Islamic nations.

Facing Islamic Nations

We must not give up the Moslem world to the devil. There is going to come a mighty move of God on Islamic enclaves. Christianity was indigenous to Turkey, Egypt, Tunisia, Sudan and Ethiopia, but these nations today are holding a wild romance with Islam. God told me that Christianity will once again sweep through these lands, even into the enclaves of Islam in the heart of the Arab lands. When Christianity was at its peak in Turkey and Egypt, no one believed Islam would ever stand a chance of entering them, let alone overrun them. But Islam overthrew Christianity in these lands. Christianity will yet powerfully and forcefully do a forward march into the heartlands of Islam.

This will not happen through wishful thinking, but through an organized, systematic, aggressive effort. We must prepare aggressive volunteer workers, men of decisive action, who are ready to sacrifice their lives to the machetes of the Moslems to save some as by fire.

We must gather enough financial and material support to set up salvation centers in nations or friendly neighboring nations where Islamic converts under the fiercest persecution can be housed, fed and taught under high security and sent back into those same nations to save their fellow brothers. It is time for war! We have been on the receiving end, but now is the time to rise up and be on the offensive. If we live on the defensive end for too long, we will be overrun and die. Courage must rise in us. We cannot love our lives under death. We must give up our lives for others. Someone laid down their life for you. The disciples did and so did Paul. What then tells you that you have the right to be too careful about yours and keep it from being spilled for another?

Churches should, as a matter of great urgency, start mobilizing aggressive prayer network fronts for core Islamic nations and peoples. Such prayer fronts should do nothing but fire prayer missiles at these nations, using the maps of such countries as contact points. If Arabs are to embrace Christianity, someone must care enough to carry the Good News of Jesus Christ to Arabs. We must start with the little knowledge and resources we have. How shall we also help to stop the spread of Islam in our predominantly "Christian" nations? We must take action.

Facing our Local/National Challenge Battle Plans

1. *First, you must know your orders* (Matthew 28:19).

We must zero in on house-to-house evangelism. Make friends and develop a relationship with your neighbor. Take him out for a ride or a run or whatever just to develop a relationship to show him your Christian love. During the usual time you take your run or participate in some sport, invite your neighbor to go with you. Do not be over-anxious to win him. You can also use the phone to get people into the fold. If we don't win them, the Buddhists, Shintos, or Moslems will. Let's rise up and rescue the perishing. We must move out of the shell of fear and take to street evangelism and door-to-door evangelism like never before.

We must get out of our la-z-boy chairs and hit the roads of evangelism and tract distribution.

2. *Follow your master* (1 Peter 2:21-23 TLB).

"This suffering is all part of the work God has given you. Christ, who suffered for you, is your example. Follow

in his steps: He never sinned, never told a lie, never answered
back when insulted; when he suffered he did not threaten to
get even; he left his case in the hands of God who always
judges fairly."

Jesus, captain of our faith, was maltreated. Why should
we think it abnormal or be afraid to be maltreated for
daring to go out on the streets and do a door-to-door solici-
tation for the Kingdom of God?

3. *Love your enemy.*

This is our intercontinental, ballistic missile (Luke 6:27-
30 TLB).

> *"Listen, all of you. Love your enemies. Do good to those*
> *who hate you. Pray for the happiness of those who curse you;*
> *implore God's blessing on those who hurt you. If someone*
> *slaps you on one cheek, let him slap the other too! If someone*
> *demands your coat, give him your shirt besides. Give what*
> *you have to anyone who asks you for it; and when things are*
> *taken away from you, don't worry about getting them back."*

What a revolutionary teaching! It contradicts everything
the human, carnal nature thinks is proper to be done to
enemies. If we are to be sons of our Father, we must realize
that obedience is better than sacrifice and to hearken more
than the fat of rams (1 Samuel 15:22). If you are willing and
obedient, you shall eat the good of the land; but if you are
stubborn and rebellious, you will be killed by your enemies
(Isaiah 1:19,20).

Unconditional love and acceptance is what Christ
teaches, nothing less. Now, that kind of love is bound to be
noticed. No wonder Christ said, *"Your strong love for each*
other will prove to the world that you are my disciples" (John
13:35 TLB).

4. *Watch your speech.*

Matthew 12:34 TLB says:

> *"You brood of snakes! How could evil men like you*
> *speak what is good and right? For a man's heart determines*
> *his speech."*

Proverbs 15:1 TLB says:

> *"A gentle answer turns away wrath, but harsh words cause quarrels."*

(I recommend that you read John chapters 4, 18 and 19.)

5. *Watch your back.*

Matthew 12:15 TLB says:

> *"But he knew what they were planning, and left the synagogue...."*

While you are busy making a frontal attack on Satan's societal evils, Satan may try to attack you from behind. Bitterness is a common wound in the culture wars of today, and it is often fatal to an effective Christian testimony.

Obey Paul's words, inspired by the wisdom of God: *"Conduct yourselves wisely toward outsiders..."* (Colossians 4:5 NRSV).

Glossary

1. Islam — Submission to the will of Allah.

2. Ramadan — The ninth month of the Muslim year, when the Qur'an was supposedly brought down to the first heaven, and now devoted to fasting.

3. Gospel — The first four books of the New Testament, telling of the birth, life, death and resurrection of Christ.

4. Spirit — The third aspect of the constitution of man.

5. Slavery — Bondage, captivity, serfdom of a person by and to a master, be it a human, religious, or spiritual master.

6. Seed — The germ, kernel, cause, origin, root, source, result of a thing.

7. Beliefs — Convictions, expectations of faith, hope, trust, or idea.

8. Animist — One who believes and practices the traditional religions (not Islam or Christianity).

9. Ghost — An apparition, phantom, shadow, or mirage of a dead person.

10. Native Doctor — One who practices an inherited demonic or herbal treatment. Is also able to give charms and render curses.

11. "Cooked"   The practice of Islam or native doctors where a person is initiated into a charm, cult, or Islam.

12. Charm   Amulet, talisman, ornament, or trinket used to effect all kinds of appeal, allurements and seductions.

13. Zombie   A moving dead man.

14. Imam   A Muslim authority in Islamic law, theology, or the man who leads the prayers. Also refers to each of the founders of the four principal sections of Islam — Shi-ites, Sufis, Sunnites.

15. Moslem   An Islamic faithful believer.

16. Curses   An affliction placed on someone to distress, grieve, torment, beset, plague, or smite.

17. "Kampe"   An underwear made of pure leather, could be made of charms.

18. Baptism   Christianity, initiation into religion or other spiritual acts.

19. Allah   Mohammed's name for the god of Islam.

20. Mohammed   The prophet and founder of Islam. Born at about A.D. 570 and died A.D. 632.

21. "Guru"   An amulet, charm, or talisman used for protection.

22. "Ja Yasin"   To call on evil omens by using combination of numbers.

23. "Ja Aya"   To create bad omens by the recitation of incantations of special mystical Qur'anic verses.

24. Incantation   Use of spells or verbal charms spoken or sung as a part of a ritual or magic, also a formula of words chanted or recited in or as if in such a ritual.

25. Concoction   To cook together by combining crude materials.

26. "Laya"   A talisman used to harm those who would harm you.

27. Luck   A force that brings "good" fortune and success.

28. Qur'an (Koran)   The Islamic book of faith, said to be the final and complete inspired word of God, transmitted to prophet Mohammed by the angel Gabriel.

29. Omen   Forewarning, indication, portent, premonition, sign of a future event.

30. Sharubutu   Hausa language word describing one who drinks the washing of ink from Koranic writings on a slate.

31. Rituals   Formality or protocol, practiced ceremonial routine.

32. Abu Bakr   The first Moslem caliph, according to Sunni Moslems.

33. Caliph   The title given to the office of the spiritual and political leadership that took over after Mohammed died.

34. Hadith   The sacred sayings of Mohammed, handed down by oral tradition, for generations after the death of Mohammed, until finally transcribed.

35. Hajj   A pilgrimage to Mecca. All Moslems are expected to make it at least once in their lifetime. Also one of the five pillars of Islam.

36. Hijrah   Mohammed's flight from Mecca to present-day Medina in A.D. 622.

37. Ka'bah   A small stone building located in the court of the largest mosque in the world located in Mecca. It is believed to contain the black stone supposedly given to Adam by the angel Gabriel and subsequently found by Abraham who allegedly built the Ka'bah.

38. Mecca   The birthplace of Mohammed. This city, located in Saudi Arabia, is considered the most holy city by the Moslems.

39. Medina   A holy city of Islam named for Mohammed. It was previously named Yathrib. It is the city to which Mohammed fled in A.D. 622.

40. Mosque   An Islamic place of prayer, worship and teaching.

41. Purdah   The restriction of women in Islam from contact with the public, which also includes keeping them locked up at home, making the houses out of bounds to visitors, and also the veiling of their head and face when mixing with people to ensure privacy against public admiration and to indicate submission to their men.

42. Salat   The Muslim daily prayer ritual. One of the five pillars of Islam.

43. Sunni Moslems   The largest Moslem sect which acknowledges the first four caliphs as Mohammed's legitimate successors.

45.	Surah (Sura)	The chapters of the Koran.
46.	Mallam	The title given to a man or a respected or honorable man. Also used for teachers.
47.	Demons	Evil, supernatural beings, adversaries.
48.	Infidel	An unbeliever in respect of a particular religion.
49.	Zakat	he levy of the rich or payment of tithes of all of one's income.
50.	Da-es-Salam	The house of peace which describes the abode of Muslims.
51.	Da-el-Harb	The house of war. The abode of non-Muslims.
52.	Sawn	Fasting in the month of Ramadan.
53.	Shahada	Bearing witness that there is no god but Allah and that Mohammed is his slave and prophet.
54.	Qiblah	The direction of prayer facing the east.
55.	Sunnah	The acts of violence in Islam which allow a Muslim to kill and be killed for Allah.
56.	Jihad	A "holy" war waged on behalf of Islam as a religious duty demanded by Allah of Mohammed.
57.	Allau Akbar	Praise God in Arabic.
58.	Trans-Atlantic	Across the Atlantic.
59.	Trans-Saharan	Across the Sahara.
60.	Arab	Arabic speaking people from the Arabian peninsula.

61.	Brotherhood	A community bound together by a common faith and way of life.
62.	Dar-al-Dhimmi	People of the book viz Christians and Jews.
63.	Witchcraft	Sorcery, voodoo, the ability to make enchantments.
64.	Gnostic	One who believes matter is evil and that emancipation comes through gnosis or knowledge.
65.	Parakletos	The Comforter, the Holy Spirit.
66.	Periklutos	The celebrated or praised.
67.	Paraclete	Greek rendering of Comforter.
68.	Munahhemana	Lifegiver, consoler, or comforter.
69.	Diabolical	Relating to or having the characteristics of the devil.

Endnotes

[1] Wilson, A. J. *Introducing Islam*. (New York: Friendship Press, 1959), p. 61.

[2] Hogben, S. J. & Kirk-Greene, A. H. M. *The Emirates of Northern Nigeria*. (London: Oxford University Press, 1966), p. 559.

[3] Boer, Jan H. *Christianity and Islam Under Colonialism in Northern Nigeria*. (Institute of Church and Society, Jos, Nigeria, 1988), pp. 41-42.

[4] *Ibid.*, p. 44.

[5] *Ibid.*, p. 45.

[6] Interview with Abubakar Salihu. December 19, 1995.

[7] Walsh, Jaria. *The Growth of the Catholic Church in the Diocese of Jos, 1907-1978*. (Ipetu-Remo,Nigeria: Ambassador Publications), p. 6.

[8] Anonymous. *The True Guidance, Part One*, "The Infallibility of Revelation and the Sins of the Prophet's Light of Life." (Villach, Austua,1904), pp. 101-102.

[9] *Ibid.*, pp. 90-94.

Other Books

by Maiwa'azi Dan Daura

Dynamics of Evangelism

The Fine Art of Making Disciples and Ministers

Developing and Releasing Your Creative Ability

Men Ablaze

How To live the Life of a New Creature

The Jealous God

God's Case Against Man

How To Take the Kingdom by Violence

The Force of Diligence

The Making of an Achiever

The Power of Flaming Desires

Called to Excellence

The Power of First Love and the Passion of Its Return

Jesus I Know, But Who Are You?

Available from your Local Christian Bookstore
or
Faith Publications
Prevailing Faith Ministries International
P. O. Box 1826, Jos, Nigeria
Tel. 011 234 73 54569
or
Higher Dimensions, Inc.
8621 South Memorial Drive
Tulsa, Oklahoma 74133-4308
U. S. A.
(918) 250-0483 or Fax (918) 250 9698